HEALTHY
INDIAN COOKING

HEALTHY INDIAN COOKING

SHEHZAD HUSAIN

PHOTOGRAPHS BY JAMES MURPHY

SERIES EDITOR
LEWIS ESSON

Bismillah – Hir – Rahmaan – Nir – Raheem
(In the name of Allah, Most Merciful, Most Kind)

Premier Books
Unit 1
Metnor Business Park
Hadrian Road
Wallsend
Tyne and Wear NE28 6HH

Healthy Indian Cooking
Copyright
© Frances Lincoln Limited 1997
Text copyright © Shehzad Husain 1997
Photographs copyright © James Murphy 1997

First Premier Books edition 1997

British Library Cataloguing in Publication Data
A catalogue record for this book is available from the British
Library
ISBN 0 7112 1216 3
Printed in Hong Kong
1 3 5 7 9 10 8 6 4 2

NOTE
Throughout the book both metric and imperial quantities
are given. Use either all metric or all imperial, as the two are
not necessarily interchangeable.

CONTENTS

Introduction   6

   Eating in the Subcontinent   6

   A Few Notes on Techniques   8

   Some Useful Utensils   9

   Some Notes on Nutrition   9

Some Indian Ingredients   10

Starters and Snacks   30

Fish and Shellfish   46

Meat and Poultry   64

Vegetarian Dishes   98

Rice and Breads   122

Salads, Side Dishes

   and Accompaniments   130

Desserts   146

Index   157

Acknowledgments   160

INTRODUCTION

With its emphasis on nutritious vegetables, pulses, rice and grains, the traditional cooking of India and Pakistan has always been, by its very nature, healthy. The meat and dairy products so dominant in Western cooking play a subsidiary role, almost as flavouring elements rather than building blocks, which means that saturated fat levels are – or should be – much lower.

I say 'should be' as there is one aspect of our tradition which tends to boost saturated fat levels and that is the use of *ghee*, clarified butter (see page 29) as the favoured cooking medium, and often even as a dressing poured over pulse dishes like *dhals*. Generally throughout this book, however, I have replaced it with healthier vegetable or olive oil, and although flavours will not be exactly the same I think the only area in which this might be obvious is in the making of bread (see Naan, page 124).

The inventive and imaginative use of spices also means that you can normally sacrifice more calorific ingredients (spices are almost entirely calorie-free!) without much noticeable loss of flavour. You will also find, as you experiment with the addition of spices to your food, that you will not need to add so much salt in your cooking.

Aromatics such as garlic, ginger and turmeric, whole grains and oil-rich nuts and seeds, as well as vegetables such as spinach, pumpkin and sweet potatoes, are all now vaunted as 'superfoods', not only blessed with ample nutrients but containing agents that actively combat disease. These are the ingredients at the heart of Indian and Pakistani cooking, making it both immensely flavourful and incredibly healthy.

EATING IN THE SUBCONTINENT

Among the questions I am most frequently asked by Westerners about Indian and Pakistani food is exactly what constitutes a typical meal and how is it served.

In my experience a typical main meal for four consists of one meat, chicken or fish dish, with one vegetarian dish or *dhal*, a rice dish and some form of bread. These would also be accompanied by a *raita* (yoghurt relish) and an assortment of chutneys or pickles. Obviously the ideal is an assortment of dishes that marry well in terms of flavour and texture (and colour). If, for example, the meat dish is a dry one, aim to serve a vegetable dish with lots of sauce.

Of course, this is a meal typical of a household of meat-eaters; the equivalent in a vegetarian household might consist of one or more vegetarian curries, one *dhal* or other pulse dish (essential as the principal source of protein), and a *raita* (again essential), together with a rice dish and some bread, and a small assortment of chutneys in the same way.

When entertaining, there would obviously be a much wider array of dishes on offer – several meat, chicken and fish or shellfish dishes, two or three vegetarian dishes and *dhals* or other pulse dishes, with lots of rice and bread and as wide a range of accompaniments as you could manage. This would normally be followed by a couple of desserts: one of the traditional Indian desserts alongside a fruit salad or simply an assortment of fresh fruit.

Unless otherwise stated, all the recipes in this book have been planned on the basis that each will form part of a typical Indian or Pakistani meal, where four people will share four or five different dishes plus rice,

bread and accompaniments in the manner described earlier. If you are planning to cook for more or fewer people, you are best advised to make more or fewer dishes (with a minimum of three), rather than scale the recipes up or down.

A FEW NOTES ON TECHNIQUES

There are very few difficult or unusual techniques involved in this book. However, the following do warrant a little bit of extra information.

GRINDING SPICES

Although ready-ground spices are a great convenience, nothing quite matches the aroma and taste of spices ground yourself as you need them (see page 10). If you start doing this, you will notice the effect in the fuller, richer and deeper flavours.

Inexpensive little electric spice grinders are now widely available, or many people use coffee grinders (but it is not a good idea to use the same one for both spices and coffee as flavour transfer tends to occur, even if you keep the machine scrupulously clean). However, I have to admit that I much prefer the good old-fashioned method of pulverizing the spices using a pestle and mortar.

You do get a coarser product this way, but I think that in the bruising process of a pestle and mortar more of the flavouring elements are retained than is the case when the spices are blitzed to a powder. If the spices are going to be given quite lengthy cooking they don't need to be ground too finely, as any larger particles will be softened before they are eaten. If, however, the dish for which they are required is, say, a rapid stir-fry, then it is wiser to grind finely or you may end up with a gritty texture.

ROASTING SPICES, SEEDS AND NUTS

As you will see in the recipes, whole spices, seeds and nuts are often first roasted, as this develops their flavours. In India this would be done on a *thawa* (see below), but it is easy to do in a dry non-stick frying pan. The pan is placed over a moderate heat and the spices, seeds or nuts stirred continuously, or the pan tilted and shaken to ensure even cooking, until the items being roasted are well coloured and aromatic. Particularly when dealing with oily seeds and nuts, you do have to keep a careful eye on the contents of the pan as they can burn very quickly if left too long over the heat.

STIR-FRYING

Although stir-frying is generally more associated with Chinese cooking, you will see that I make considerable use of the technique as it keeps a higher proportion of the nutrients (and flavour and texture) of ingredients. The technique could not be easier to master, but it is surprising how alien some Western cooks find its principles and practice.

In general all that you have to remember is that the ingredients are added in stages, grouping together at each stage all those items which will take the same time to cook, so that at the end of the process everything is cooked to the right degree at the same time. This can mean, however, that there are no obvious visual signs of when you have reached the right stage to add the next batch of ingredients as what is in the pan is still in the process of cooking, so you have to use your instincts and learn from experience.

Preparation is critical in stir-frying. Get all your ingredients peeled and chopped before you start cooking (don't do this too far ahead or you will lose freshness and nutrients).

It helps to group together – say, in separate bowls – the ingredients which are going to be added at each stage. Also cut each ingredient into pieces which are roughly the same size, so they will cook uniformly.

As you will see, I usually start the process by stir-frying the flavouring ingredients, such as spices, seeds and curry leaves for example, for less than a minute until they are aromatic, before I add anything else, However, I will often also add chopped or sliced onion at this early stage as onions usually need to be cooked until they are quite soft.

Often very delicate items, such as green leaves or fresh herbs, are added at the very last minute and stirred in briefly just to wilt them before the dish is served.

For the actual method of frying, it is best to stir the contents of a pan in repeated sweeping backward and forward semi-circular movements to ensure that all the food in contact with the bottom of the pan is stirred up to prevent it catching.

SOME USEFUL UTENSILS

THAWA
This round, slightly concave iron plate or griddle is used for making bread such as *chapati*. A good heavy non-stick frying pan will give satisfactory results.

KADAHI
This pan is very similar to a wok, although slightly heavier and with a ring-shaped handle on either side. A wok or a good heavy deepish frying pan will work perfectly well in its place.

SOME NOTES ON NUTRITION

The figures given in the nutritional information panel that accompanies each recipe are per serving and have been rounded off to the nearest whole number. Optional ingredients have not been included and the figures are based on the largest number of suggested servings.

The ranges given for fat, protein and carbohydrate content are based on the proportion each makes of the total calorie content as follows.

Total fat:	Low = under 25%
	Medium = 25-33%
	High = over 33%
Saturated fat:	Low = under 5%
	Medium = 5-10%
	High = over 10%
Protein:	Low = under 15%
	Medium = 15-20%
	High = over 20%
Carbohydrate:	Low = under 50%
	Medium = 50-60%
	High = over 60%

Please note that such a system can occasionally produce results that seem surprising when not viewed in a wider context. For example, a salad or *dhal* made with a mere 1 or 2 tablespoons of oil can have a very low overall calorie count, so its fat content reads as 'high' in this system. However, were that dish to be analysed together with an accompanying bowl of rice, the increase in total calories could reduce the level of fat to 'medium' or even 'low'.

SOME INDIAN INGREDIENTS

SPICES

Nothing characterizes Indian cooking more than its vivid and imaginative use of dried spices, possibly because so many of the plants from which the spices are derived are either native to the subcontinent or grow there well. Indeed, India is now the world's largest exporter of spices.

Of course, 'spicy' doesn't have to mean 'hot'. Just as salt and pepper levels are adjusted to suit personal taste in European cooking, the quantities of salt and chillies in Indian and Pakistani cuisine may be varied without in any way compromising the authenticity of the dish. Don't let anyone bully you into eating or using quantities of chilli that you find so excessive that you cannot really sense – let alone enjoy – the flavours underlying them.

Using spices

There are many ways of employing spices. You can use them whole, ground, roasted, fried or mixed with yoghurt to marinate meat and poultry. One spice can completely alter the flavour of a dish and combinations of several in varying proportions can produce totally different colours and textures.

Many of the recipes in this book call for ground spices, which are generally available in supermarkets as well as in Indian and Pakistani food shops. In India, we almost always buy whole spices and grind them ourselves, and there is no doubt that freshly ground spices do make a noticeable difference to the taste (and, of course, powders are too easily adulterated). It cannot be denied that it is more convenient, and quicker, to use ready-ground spices – but the flavours they impart will not be as lively.

When buying spices, always get them from a shop that you are sure has a rapid turnover, otherwise they may have been languishing on a shelf for years and have lost all their flavour – or worse still developed a mustiness or off-flavour that will actually mar any dish in which they are used. Ready-ground spices in particular only have a shelf-life of a matter of months. Keep all spices in a tightly closed jar in a cool and dry place away from sunlight (those kitchen spice racks of clear bottles sitting on window sills are actually not a good idea at all).

For some of the recipes, the spices need to be roasted. In India this is done on a *thawa* (see page 9), but instead you can use a heavy, ideally cast-iron, frying pan. No water or oil is added to the spices, they are simply dry-roasted whole while the pan is shaken to stop them burning (see page 8). Stop when they are lightly coloured and highly aromatic.

Amchoor *Mangifera indica*

Also known as mango powder and sometimes spelt *amchur*, this flavouring, popular in North and East India, is made from unripe mangoes which have been sliced and sun-dried, then ground to a powder. It is mainly used to impart a tart fruity sourness to fish and vegetable dishes, although it also appears in some breads and pastries. It is sometimes sprinkled on meat and poultry to tenderize them. Mangoes are regarded as system cleansers and as kidney tonics.

Cardamom *Elettaria cardamomum, Elaichi*

Native to the tropical jungles of southern India, cardamom is arguably the second most expensive spice, after saffron. The pods can be used with or without their husks and have a slightly pungent but very aromatic taste. They come in three varieties: green, white and black. The green and white pods (the white are simply green pods which have been bleached for the sake of appearance) can be used for both sweet and savoury dishes or to flavour rice. The black, which are not true cardamom but from plants of the related *Amomum* and *Afromomum* genus, are cheaper, coarser and

less aromatic, and only used for savoury dishes. Cardamom's essential oils are particularly volatile, so it is better to buy the intact pods and use them whole, where appropriate, or crush them for the inner seeds as required. Cardamom pods are chewed as breath fresheners and digestive aids, and they are also said to sharpen the mind.

CHILLI *Capsicum frutescens*

Dried red chillies (*sabath sookhi laal mirch*) are sold whole in some supermarkets and in most Asian stores. They are extremely fiery and should be used with caution; their effect can be toned down slightly by slitting them open and shaking out the seeds. Dried chillies are usually fried in oil before use. When handling dried chillies be careful not to touch any sensitive parts of your body – or of anyone else's – and wash your hands immediately afterwards. Crushed dried chillies are also sold, but tend not to have the potency and flavour of the whole pods. Chilli powder (*laal mirch*) and cayenne pepper can be very fiery, when fresh, and

should be used with caution. However, these ground products have even less potency than crushed dried flakes.

CINNAMON *Cinnamomum verum, Dhalchini*

This most warming and familiar of spices is made from the bark of a tree of the laurel family that is native to Sri Lanka. It is sold as sticks, which are actually quills of rolled bark, or ground to a powder. When I use whole lengths of sticks in cooking I like to leave them in the dish when serving as they look so attractive; if your guests are unfamiliar with Indian food, however, do warn them that the cinnamon should not be eaten. Cinnamon is held to be a natural system cleanser and an aid to digestion. It is also antibacterial and helps relieve congestion.

CLOVES *Eugenia caryophylus, Laung*

Cloves are the dried unopened flower buds of a small evergreen tree native to the Moluccas, or Spice Islands, now part of Indonesia. Cloves lend their warming pungency to many sweet and savoury dishes and are usually added whole in Indian cooking. Like cinnamon sticks, they are often removed after cooking (hence the common European practice of studding onions with cloves – they are then easier to remove). The spike of a whole clove is also sometimes used to secure a rolled betel leaf for serving as a breath freshener after an Indian meal. Look for cloves that have paler crowns than spikes and which snap cleanly, possibly exuding a little oil when pressed. Ground cloves form part of most *garam masala* mixtures (see opposite). The essential oil from cloves has long been used as a natural pain-killer, particularly against toothache. It also aids digestion and relieves flatulence.

CORIANDER SEEDS *Coriandrum sativum, Dhania*

The aromatic brown seeds of the coriander plant have a pungent, slightly lemony flavour which is widely used in meat, fish and poultry dishes. They are available whole, coarsely ground or powdered. The ground versions do lose their potency very quickly.

Try to buy Indian coriander seeds, which are sweeter, paler and more elongated than more readily available Moroccan seeds. Coriander seeds are noted for their beneficial effect on the digestive system.

CUMIN *Cuminum cyminum*

There are two main varieties of cumin seeds: the more common light brown type and the black. The smaller, thinner black cumin seeds (*shah zeera*), native to India and Pakistan, have a stronger and sweeter aromatic flavour, almost akin to caraway. Used to flavour curries and rice, they are available from most good Asian stores, but do tend to be more expensive than ordinary cumin. The flavour of cumin, like that of most seeds, is greatly improved by roasting or frying before use. Ground cumin (*safaid zeera*) has a musty smell and is widely used for flavouring lentils and vegetable curries. Ground cumin is a constituent of most curry powders and of *garam masala* (see right).

FENNEL SEEDS *Foeniculum vulgare, Sonfe*

Very similar in appearance to white cumin, these seeds have a sweet aniseed taste and are used to flavour some curries and many vegetarian and fish dishes. They can also be chewed (like betel leaves and cardamom) after a spicy meal. Fennel seeds are said to help the body digest fatty foods and also to help suppress the appetite.

FENUGREEK *Trigonella foenum-graecum, Methi*

The flavour of the whole dried flat yellow seeds is almost unpalatably astringent, but improves, when the seeds are lightly fried, to that of a slightly bitter celery or lovage. Ground fenugreek seeds are an ingredient in many curry powders and, as they are relatively cheap, they tend to

predominate in poorer-quality blends. Rich in vitamin A, fenugreek is considered to have the ability to cleanse the body of toxins.

GARAM MASALA

Meaning 'hot spices', these aromatic mixtures of spices can either be made up at home from freshly ground spices or bought ready-made. There is no set formula, but a typical mixture might include black cumin seeds, peppercorns, cloves, cinnamon and black cardamom seeds.

To make your own, gently roast in a dry frying pan over moderate heat until aromatic a 2.5-cm / 1-inch piece of cinnamon stick with 3 cloves, 3 black peppercorns, the seeds from 2 black cardamom pods and 2 teaspoons of black cumin seeds. Allow them to cool and then grind them together. If you wish, multiply the quantities, grind and store in an airtight jar for future use.

If buying commercial ready-made *garam masala*, note that the pastes keep their potency longer than the powders.

Garam masala tends to be added at a fairly late stage in cooking, or even as a garnish, to get the most benefit from the aroma of the spices.

GINGER *Zingiber officinale, Sonth*
Ground dried ginger is used as well as fresh in Indian cooking. As a result of its long association with the baking of breads and biscuits in the West, it is readily available in most supermarkets and food shops.

MUSTARD SEEDS *Brassica nigra, B. juncea, Sarson ke beenji rai*
These seeds, either black or yellow, are round and sharp-flavoured. They are used for flavouring curries and pickles and develop a delicious nutty taste when first fried in oil. Mustard seeds stimulate the appetite and are said to be good for the skin.

NUTMEG *Mystica fragrans, Jaifal*
The nutmeg is the dried kernel of the fruit of a flowering evergreen tree native to the Moluccas. Its rich, sweet, warm and aromatic flavour is quite fugitive, so try to avoid the ready-ground powders and grate whole nutmegs as and when you need them. Nutmeg is traditionally thought to have general tonic properties, especially for the digestive system, heart, brain and reproductive organs.

ONION SEEDS *Allium cepa, Kalongi*
Black in colour and triangular in shape, these seeds are used for both pickles and vegetable curries.

PAPRIKA *Capsicum tetragonum*
This powder, made from dried varieties of sweet red pepper (mostly pericarp), is known in the West as a hot-flavoured spice but is very mild in comparison to chilli pepper. There are sweet and hot varieties of the powder, usually depending on whether or not the peppers' seeds have been included. Ubiquitous in the cuisines of Spain and Eastern Europe, paprika is occasionally used in Indian cooking.

PEPPERCORNS *Piper nigrum*
The peppercorn is one of the oldest spices known to humankind and is native to the tropical forests of India's Malabar Coast. After salt, pepper is probably the most common flavouring in both Western and Indian cooking. Peppercorns are the tiny berries of a vining shrub; they are picked when fully developed but still unripe.

Black peppercorns are sun-dried; white peppercorns are first soaked in water so that the outer skin may be washed off to reveal the pale inner core prior to sun-drying. As the flavour is mostly held in the outer skin, while the pungency lies in the inner core, white pepper is 'hotter' than black but with a more subtle flavour. It is often favoured in dishes with pale sauces, to avoid speckling.

Green peppercorns (*badi mirch*) are the freshly harvested berries, which are normally preserved either in vinegar or brine, although they may be freeze-dried or commercially dehydrated. They have a much fresher, almost caper-like, flavour.

Red or pink peppercorns come from a totally unrelated plant, the Brazilian pepper (*Schinus terebinthifolius*). These have little pungency but a sweet citrusy flavour and, of course, they look highly decorative. Mixtures of all four types of peppercorn are available and these give an interesting blend of flavours and pungency.

Pepper stimulates the appetite and digestion, encourages perspiration and also has considerable antioxidant and antibacterial properties.

POMEGRANATE SEEDS *Punica granatum, Anar dana*
It is said that the fruit with which Eve tempted Adam in the Garden of Eden was not an apple at all, but a pomegranate; and its name can be translated as 'apple with seeds'. The

fruit and its seeds are a potent symbol of fertility in many cultures. The fresh seeds of the fruit are a popular garnish in Middle Eastern cooking and the dried seeds, resembling small raisins, are valued for their sweet-and-sour flavour in Indian cooking. Ground dried pomegranate seeds are used as a souring agent in Northern Indian cooking, particularly in their chutneys and vegetable and pulse dishes.

Poppy Seeds *Papaver somniferum, Khush khush*

These are the dried seeds of the opium poppy; although opium is derived from the unripe seed pod, the seeds do not contain any of the drug. Seeds of the variety more common in India are yellow in colour rather than the blue-grey of the seeds so long familiar in Western baking. Their delicious nutty flavour is always better when the seeds have first been roasted. They are used, often whole, to flavour curries. Ground poppy seeds are sometimes used as a thickening agent.

Saffron *Crocus sativus, Zafran*

This, the world's most expensive spice, is made from the stigmas of the saffron crocus, which is native to Asia Minor. The production of each 30 g / 1 oz of saffron requires around five thousand stigmas, and each crocus bears only three stigmas, which need to be hand-picked at precisely the right stage of development. Fortunately, only a small quantity of saffron is needed to flavour or colour a dish, whether sweet or savoury. Saffron is sold both as whole strands and in powder form. It has a beautiful flavour and fragrance. To bring out the flavour, saffron is often first very lightly roasted and then soaked in milk. Beware of poor-quality or adulterated saffron which can have a disagreeably bitter flavour.

Sesame Seeds *Sesamum indicum, Thill*

The flat, cream-coloured unhulled seeds of an Asian and African annual, sesame seeds have been cultivated since antiquity for their abundant oil. Their full nutty flavour is best developed by roasting and they are used to flavour some curries. Look for bright-looking seeds to use; older seeds in which the oils have gone rancid develop a muddy grey appearance.

Tamarind *Tamarindus indica, Imli*

The tamarind plant, also known as the Indian date, grows freely in India and its dried black pods are sticky and very sour-tasting. The sweet-and-sour fruity flavour is very familiar to Westerners as the basis for Worcestershire sauce. In India it is used in many curries, especially with lentils and vegetables, and chutneys. Tamarind has to be soaked in hot water to extract the flavour. Lemon juice, though much weaker, is often used as a substitute. Nowadays tamarind can be bought in paste form in jars: mix the paste with a little water to get it to a runny consistency before use. Tamarind is noted for its mild laxative effect.

Turmeric *Curcuma longa, Haled*

The turmeric plant is related to ginger and, as with ginger, it is the rhizome or underground stem which is valued for its flavour. Seldom available fresh in the West, it is usually sold dried and most commonly ground. The bright yellow, bitter-tasting spice is used mainly for colour (it is often used as a cheaper substitute for saffron) rather than flavour, although its musky taste is important in most curry powders. It has significant powers to aid digestion and as an antiseptic and antifungal, and is often used to treat wounds, but be careful of it as it stains very easily.

HERBS

Perhaps because of the overwhelmingly powerful presence of spices in Indian food – and the long cooking that these often need to develop flavour – herbs are not nearly as important as they are in Western cooking, or even in the cuisines of neighbouring cultures , for example those of Southeast Asia.

Nevertheless, several herbs are fairly common in Indian cooking, principally because they marry well with other frequently used ingredients.

BAY LEAVES *Laurus nobilis, Tez patta*

One of the most ancient of herbs used in cooking, the leaves of the bay or laurel tree are sold fresh and dried. Although the crushed dried leaves are sometimes included in some garam masala mixtures, bay is not very widely used in curries.

CORIANDER *Coriandrum sativum, Hara dhania*

This beautifully fragrant herb is used in Indian cooking much as parsley is in the West, both as an ingredient and as a garnish. Its zesty flavour marries well with chillies and for

this reason it has been adopted in most cuisines which also feature chilli heat. I must admit to being an addict and you will see that it features in most of my savoury recipes.

Until recently fresh coriander was relatively difficult to find in the West; in recent years, however, it has become familiar in our market stalls and supermarkets. In appearance it is fairly similar to flat-leaved parsley, but it is fortunately made easier to recognize as it is often sold with its roots intact, as these and the stems are useful for flavouring stocks and vegetable and pulse dishes. The presence of the roots also makes coriander much easier to keep in water than most cut herbs.

CURRY LEAVES *Murraya koenigii, Kari patta*
These are similar in appearance to bay leaves but very different in flavour, with a distinct curry-like aroma. They can be bought both dried and occasionally fresh (unfortunately the dried leaves have considerably less flavour than the fresh), and are principally used to flavour lentil dishes and vegetable curries.

FENUGREEK *Trigonella foenum-graecum, Methi*
Fresh fenugreek, sold in bunches, has very small leaves and is used to flavour both meat and vegetarian dishes. The dried leaves are also used.

MINT *Mentha* spp., *Podina*
The fresh taste of mint leaves has long been appreciated in many cuisines and it is perhaps this freshness which has kept it popular in the cooking of India, particularly in chutneys and raitas. It also works very well in tandem with coriander and goes especially well with ingredients popular in Indian dishes like lamb and yoghurt. Dried mint leaves unfortunately don't seem to retain much of the power of the fresh, one reason why I favour using commercial mint sauces as a flavouring if fresh leaves are not available.

OTHER AROMATICS
The fresh vegetables in this section are mostly used like herbs and spices, for their flavouring properties, but are generally sold on vegetable counters.

As ginger and garlic are used very frequently in curries, and it takes time and effort to peel and chop them every time, I suggest you take about 225 g / 8 oz of each, soak them overnight (this makes them easier to peel), peel them and grind them separately in a food processor, adding a little water to form a pulp. They can then be stored in airtight containers in the refrigerator for about a month.

Alternatively, for the recipes where I specify one teaspoon of garlic or ginger pulp, you can substitute two finely chopped garlic cloves or one shredded 1-cm / ½-in slice of ginger. There are also many good-quality commercial ready-made ginger and garlic sauces which can deliver much of the flavour of these aromatics with little or no effort, and I freely admit to using them when cooking in a hurry without any chance of pre-preparation. They make excellent store-cupboard stand-bys.

CHILLIES *Capsicum frutescens*
Fresh green chillies (*hari mirch*) and their riper red counterparts are used in Indian cooking both as an ingredient and as a garnish. As well as imparting their own richly aromatic flavour and their heat, they also seem to have the power to bring out the flavours of ingredients around them. Originally from South America, chillies are now mostly grown in Africa and Indonesia. Look for crisp and firm peppers, with no wrinkles or blemishes.

Those used to the pungency of chillies tend to cook the entire pepper, even when chopped or sliced. In this book I only specify deseeding chillies where I think it is necessary. However, those less inured to chilli heat are probably best advised to remove the seeds and the pale membrane to which they are attached, as these are the hottest parts. As

with dried peppers, take great care when handling peppers not to touch the face or other sensitive parts of the body, and wash your hands well immediately afterwards.

Fresh chillies are packed with vitamins A, B and C (in fact, weight for weight, they are six times richer in vitamin C than oranges). They are also potent stimulants to the system, are highly antibacterial and help normalize blood pressure.

GARLIC *Allium sativum, Lassun*

The garlic plant is a member of the lily family, the bulbs or heads of which have been used to flavour food since ancient times. Garlic is frequently used in curries, especially in conjunction with ginger, and whole cloves are sometimes added to lentil dishes. Garlic powder is useful for adding to flour to make a spicy coating for food.

As long as garlic has been known it has been valued as much for its medicinal properties as for its flavour, and today it is now hailed as one of the 'superfoods' with active health-giving properties. It is antiseptic and powerfully antibacterial when raw, and even when cooked it helps the body eliminate toxins and lowers cholesterol.

GINGER *Zingiber officinale, Adrak*

Although fresh ginger is usually called root ginger, the part of the plant that we use to flavour food is actually a rhizome, or thickened underground stem. Fresh ginger is one of the most popular and ancient of flavourings used in India, and is an important ingredient in many curries. For Indian dishes, ginger is usually peeled and then cut into matchstick shreds, or used as a pulp (see page 17).

Ginger is a potent stimulant and aids the digestive processes. Research has also shown that it alleviates travel sickness and vertigo and it has indeed been a folk treatment for these ailments for centuries. Infusions of ginger are also recommended against colds and sore throats.

VEGETABLES

AUBERGINE *Baingun, Brinjal*

The aubergine, a member of the same family as the potato and tomato, is much favoured particularly in the vegetarian cooking of its native India, because of its adaptability, fine meaty texture and ability both to absorb and to blend strong added flavours.

Look for well-rounded specimens with taut unwrinkled and unblemished skins. Leave the skins on; they are quite digestible and highly nutritious. The aubergine is rich in bioflavinoids which help arterial renewal and prevent blood clotting. It is also thought to be helpful in preventing some forms of cancer.

CAULIFLOWER *Phool gobi*

This close relative of the cabbage and cousin to broccoli is again a favourite of Indian vegetarian cooking because of its fine texture and ability to take up flavours. Like cabbage, cauliflower must not be overcooked or it starts to break down, giving off the characteristic sulphurous odour. Buy only fresh-looking cauliflowers with firm curds, ideally still with unwilted leaves attached. Many people go for a perfect white colour; but, in fact, the greenish varieties cook faster and often have a better flavour. Like all members of the cabbage family, the cauliflower is rich in the antioxidants that help prevent cancer. It is also richer in calcium and contains more folic acid than almost any other vegetable, so earning itself the epithet 'vegetable liver'.

DOODHI *Lagenaria siceria*

Also known as *lokhi* or bottle gourd, this smooth pale green variety of gourd, reminiscent of a large cucumber, is very important in the cooking of India. The firm but tender flesh of young specimens is well flavoured, with hints of cucumber and courgette, but they do become unpleasantly bitter and tough when old. They are usually peeled before use and any large seeds removed.

GREEN BEAN *Sem*

There are literally hundreds of varieties of green beans (*Phaseolus vulgaris*) cultivated all over the world; though they may vary in colour and dimension, they all have much the same characteristics. Generally the firmer and brighter they are the better, and they should snap cleanly and crisply when broken (hence their alternative name 'snap beans'). They need to be topped and tailed prior to cooking. Most varieties now sold have been bred to be stringless, but if you encounter some types that have tough strings these must also be removed. Brief preliminary blanching also helps fix the beans' bright colour.

MOOLI

Also known as daikon, this large pale radish looks more like a big smooth parsnip and has a wonderful sharp peppery flavour. It is also much richer in vitamin C than the little red radishes common in the West. Buy only firm moolis that seem heavy for their size; they keep well for some time in the refrigerator, so don't worry about buying one that is bigger than you need for one dish. They are also excellent aids to the digestion, particularly of starchy foods like pulses and potatoes, and thought to help prevent cancer.

OKRA *Bhindi*

Also known as ladies' fingers, these are the immature seed pods of a small bush related to the cotton plant and native to Africa. When fresh, they have a wonderful rich flavour and are filled with edible seeds in mucilaginous juices which act as a natural thickening agent for any dish in which they are used. Look for smallish firm glossy pods with no hints of browning at the tips. If using them whole, be careful when removing the stalk end not to break into the interior of the pod or you will lose the juices. Okra are highly nutritious, rich in vegetable protein and folic acid, and the juices are held to soothe the gut.

SPINACH *Saag*

Rather than the common spinach (*Spinacea oleracea*) familiar in the West, the leaves used in India are most likely to be 'Indian spinach' from a member of the unrelated mallow family, Malabar Nightshade (*Basella alba* and *B. rubra*). They are very similar, so ordinary spinach produces much the same results. Although highly nutritious, rich in vitamin A and minerals (especially iron and calcium), spinach is also high in oxalic acid. When cooked, this has the effect of inhibiting the body's absorption of some nutrients, so avoid eating too much cooked spinach at one sitting or having it as part of several meals in succession.

SWEET POTATO *Ipomoea batatas, Shakar kand*

These tubers of a member of the convolvulus family native to Central America are now grown all over the tropics. There are several varieties with yellowish, pinkish, red or purple skins, but they fall into two main types: one with drier mealier yellowish flesh and the other with softer more moist white flesh. The latter have a sweeter flavour and are more popular in Asia. They are cooked much like potatoes, mostly boiled or baked in their skins. Choose plump specimens with unwrinkled skins. Sweet potatoes are highly nutritious and easily digested. They are held to be good for the circulation and to help eliminate toxins.

PULSES AND DHALS

BLACK-EYE BEANS *Lobhia*

These cream-coloured beans get their name from the irregular black spot along their stem ends. With a fine buttery texture and a nutty, smoky flavour, they are a useful pulse in that they cook quickly and require no pre-soaking. They are readily available from most good supermarkets. High in protein, they are an important food in India.

CHICKPEAS *Chhole*

These irregularly shaped buff-coloured peas, looking a little like hazelnuts, have a full nutty flavour and keep their shape

well when cooked. Chickpeas do, however, need lengthy soaking and cooking, after which the outer skins have to be removed. Fortunately, the readily available canned chickpeas have quite a good flavour and an excellent texture (and retain a considerable amount of nutrients). In India, roasted dried chickpeas (*bhoonay chanay*) are commonly sold in packets as a snack.

KIDNEY BEANS *Rajma*

There is a wide variety of these highly nutritious beans, all of which keep their shape and buttery texture well when they are cooked. All members of this family, however, contain toxins in the skin which need to be eliminated by 10-15 minutes' initial rapid boiling before the long slow simmering until tender. As with chickpeas, canned red kidney beans are a boon, as they eliminate the necessity for all the lengthy preparation and cooking, yet still have a good flavour and texture and retain a substantial percentage of the nutrients.

CHANA DHAL

Very similar in appearance to yellow split peas, with slightly less shiny grains, this is actually a small variety of chickpea. It has a sweet 'meaty' flavour and accounts for about 50% of the pulse crop in the subcontinent. It may be bought from Indian or Pakistani grocers, but yellow split peas may be substituted if you can't obtain it.

MASOOR DHAL

These small, round and salmon-coloured split lentils, which turn yellow on cooking, are stocked by all supermarkets, labelled simply 'lentils' or 'red lentils'. Lentils do not require pre-soaking before cooking, but it is a good idea to pick them over carefully as they can easily hide small stones among their number. Lentils are highly nutritious and easily digested.

MOONG DHAL

These tear-drop-shaped yellow split lentils are more popular in northern India than in the south.

TOOR DHAL

This small orangey-red pulse also known as *tur* or *arhar*, is the pigeon pea. It is almost exclusively used in the south and west of India as it will usually not grow in the colder north. It is very popular as it is light, easy to cook and highly digestible.

URID DHAL

Though very similar in shape and size to moong dhal, these lentils are white and a little drier when cooked. As with moong dhal, they are more popular amongst northern Indians.

FRUIT

GUAVA *Amrood*

This pear-like fruit of a tree of the myrtle family is native to the Americas but is now to be found all over the world, growing in both tropical and subtropical areas. The fragrant grainy flesh has something of the aroma of quince, but with a sweet-and-sour exoticism that produces memorable sorbets, fruit butters and jams. Look for large guavas with a pale skin that gives slightly to pressure, and a pleasing floral scent (overripe guavas have an overpowering aroma). The guava is said to be good for the bones and for the lymphatic system.

MANGO *Aam*

A good well-ripened mango must rank among the most delicious of fruits and it is no accident that the gift of mangoes is a symbol of friendship in India. Unfortunately, all too often mangoes sold in the West have been picked too early and may never ripen or are of a variety that is naturally fibrous and may even possess a flavour which hints of paint thinner. You have to be very picky – even when buying green unripe fruit for cooking – and should be prepared to pay a little over the odds; after all, good mangoes are expensive even in the places where they are grown. Look for a good variety like the Alphonso and, generally (dare I say it?) mangoes from the subcontinent are among the best. Buy heavy firm fruit which just yields to pressure and has a fine perfumed scent, with no hint of fermentation in it.

The mango stone is a real 'clinger'. To get the flesh most easily from a ripe mango, cut down through the fruit lengthwise on either side of the stone. Take the two half-round sections you have removed and cut a lattice into the flesh, then press the outside of the curved skins to turn these sections inside out, producing easily removable cubes of flesh on the other side. Any flesh still clinging to the stone may be sliced off, or nibbled off as a treat. Mangoes are regarded as great systemic cleansers, good for the body, skin and kidneys.

PAPAYA *Papai*

Also known as pawpaw, the papaya is a native of the tropical Americas but came to India before the end of the sixteenth century. As the trees are particularly generous bearers, they are an important part of the economy in many tropical areas. The large oval or pear-shaped fruits resemble melons. Their perfumed orangey-yellow flesh is delicious when ripe, and the black seeds have a peppery flavour so are often used as a condiment or garnish. As with mangoes, unripe papayas are sometimes cooked like vegetables. Again, buy fruit that feels heavy for its size, that is just beginning to soften and that bears no trace of green on the skin. Papayas are rich in the enzyme papain, which breaks down proteins, so they are used as a meat tenderizer, in marinades. This means that they can also help in the digestion of a protein-rich meal. Papaya has considerable powers as a general cleanser and detoxifier. It is said to keep the eyes and skin bright, and some people use the juices to try to remove freckles.

PINEAPPLE *Ananas*

After the banana, the pineapple is probably the most familiar of tropical fruits in the West. Indeed the wonderful idiosyncratic pine-cone shape of the fruit has been a popular decorative device in Europe for centuries. Native to the West Indies, it is now grown all over the tropics, with Hawaii the major producer.

Pineapples ripen very rapidly, but will simply not ripen once picked, so be careful when buying them; they should have a full floral scent and the little leaves at the stalk end should come away with ease. Before preparing a pineapple, stand it upside down for about 30 minutes to allow the juices to redistribute. Cut off the leafy crown and cut the fruit across into thick slices. Remove the skin around the edge of the slices and then cut out the woody discs of internal core.

Pineapples are also rich in a protein-digesting enzyme called bromelin, so they are used in marinades and to help in the digestion of meat-rich meals. Bromelin also curdles milk or cream and will prevent gelatine-based jellies from setting, so when making jellies including pineapple use agar agar instead. Pineapples are very rich in vitamin C and the bromelin literally digests microbes.

NUTS

Almond *Badaam*

The almond is one of the most important nuts used in cooking worldwide. Related to the peach and the apricot, it is thought to have originated in the Middle East and has certainly been a favourite in Arab sweet and savoury cooking for thousands of years. There are two types of the nut: bitter almonds and sweet almonds. The former have more flavour, but are poisonous when raw. The two types of nut are often used together in cooked dishes, as the bitter almonds bring out the flavour of their sweet cousins.

Almonds are highly nutritious and particularly rich in folic acid. Increasingly, they are also thought to have considerable anti-cancer properties.

CASHEW *Kaju*

These delicious long white nuts with a distinctive texture are related to the mango and pistachio. Native to Brazil, they were brought to Goa by the Portuguese and now India rivals Brazil as a producer. As the shell of the fresh nut exudes a blistering oil, we usually only ever see the dried shelled nuts for sale. Cashews are rich in minerals, particularly zinc.

COCONUT *Khopra, Narial*

Because of its abundance and versatility, the coconut plays an important part in the cooking of most of India, and southern Asia in general. The mature nut is cracked open (do this carefully, as the juice inside can make a refreshing drink), the flesh is separated into chunks and the skin is removed. The flesh is then usually grated to a pulp, and this may be used as it is (sometimes after brief toasting), or frozen for future use. More often than not, it is used to make coconut milk or cream, by soaking it in hot water. The first soaking process produces the thicker 'cream' and subsequent soakings give the thinner 'milk'.

Of course, dried (or desiccated) shredded coconut flesh has been readily available in the West for many years, as it is popular in baking and the making of sweets. This can be used to make coconut cream and milk by soaking it as described above. Canned coconut cream and milk is now readily available and you may also find frozen coconut cream and milk; these make perfectly acceptable substitutes, although they often contain additives.

Because the fats in coconut are more highly saturated than in almost anything else in the vegetable kingdom, coconut and coconut products have to be used in moderation by anyone intent on enjoying a healthy diet. In this book I have tried to reduce the quantities used considerably. However, the nut is totally without cholesterol (unlike similarly saturated animal fats), is rich in iodine and iron, and is one of the best sources of medium-chain fats, thought to play a very important role in the metabolizing of fats in general. Indeed, many coconut-based drugs make use of this property.

PINE NUTS *Chilghozay*

The seeds of many types of pine tree are edible. Perhaps the best-known in the West come from the Mediterranean stone pine (*Pinus pinea*), which are very similar to the pine nuts used in the cooking of eastern India. The pine cones are gathered in autumn and winter and stored until summer, when they are dried in the sun. The nuts then shake readily out of the cones, although nowadays the processing is mostly done by machinery. The very oily nuts have a lovely buttery taste and texture, and are best lightly roasted prior to use. Pine nuts contain a broad range of nutrients and are among the richest sources of protein by weight in the vegetable kingdom.

PISTACHIO *Pista*

These small pale- to dark-green nuts (the darker the green, the better the flavour), with an evocative slightly resinous flavour, are native to Asia but are also popular in most Middle-eastern and Mediterranean countries. Their use is mostly associated with the cooking of Islamic cultures, and they are widely used in Indian desserts. For cooking, be careful not to buy the salty type sold in their shells as a snack, but the shelled and unsalted nuts sold in packets at all Indian and Pakistani grocers. Pistachios are said to help purify the blood and promote liver and kidney activity.

RICE AND FLOURS

BASMATI RICE

The average southern Indian is said to be able to recognize at least twenty varieties of rice by sight. In this book, however, I have only suggested the use of (polished white) basmati rice – even for my rice pudding. This long-grain rice grown in the Himalayan foothills is aged for about a year and has a wonderful rich aromatic flavour and fine texture. It also has the advantage of cooking in about 10 minutes, although it benefits from lengthy rinsing – in a sieve under running water or in several fresh bowls of water – and/or soaking prior to cooking. As it tends to elongate during cooking (rather than plump up) and contains less starch than other long-grain varieties, it also produces nice separate grains. More than anything, however, I just love it for its delicious flavour! White rice also retains quite a substantial proportion of the grain's nutrients, particularly its proteins.

CHAPATI FLOUR

Also known as *ata*, this very finely ground wholemeal flour may be bought at any Indian or Pakistani shop. It is used to make *chapati*, *paratha* and *poori*. Finely sieved ordinary wholemeal flour may also be used for Indian breads.

GRAM FLOUR

Also known as *besan* or *besun*, this fine flour is made from chana dhal (see page 23). It is used to make *pakoras* and also as a binding agent and to make batters for coating fried food. A combination of gram flour and ordinary wholemeal flour makes a delicious Indian bread called *besun ki roti*.

DAIRY PRODUCTS

GHEE

This is the clarified butter which is the principal cooking medium of India. In this book I have eliminated it from my recipes, except for a little in the Naan recipe on page 124, and replaced it with olive oil or corn oil, both of which have a much lower saturated fat content. Because of all the other strong flavours in the food, I think the difference will only possibly be noticed in the bread recipes, where the texture and flavour of the ghee is such a part of the experience.

PANIR

This is the fresh curd cheese, usually made at home, used in many ways all over India and Pakistan. See the recipe on page 140.

YOGHURT *Raita*

This soured milk product is used in India in innumerable ways, just like cream in European cuisine. When adding yoghurt to curries, to give it a thick creamy texture, I always whip it first with a fork and then add it gradually so that it does not curdle. Yoghurt in marinades also helps to tenderize meat.

Always use plain unsweetened un-set yoghurt, preferably bio for its healthy cultures. I do sometimes use low-fat *fromage frais* and *crème fraîche*, but one of the real advantages of using yoghurt in cooking is that low-fat varieties don't seem to lose flavour in the way that low-fat versions of other dairy products tend to.

MISCELLANEOUS

KEWRA WATER

This clear delicately scented liquid, made from the exquisitely scented flowers of the screwpine tree (*Pandanus odoratissimus*), is used to flavour many sweet dishes and some poultry and rice dishes. It can be bought in most Indian and Pakistani shops.

ROSE WATER

Rose water is made from essence of rose petals and is a popular flavouring in Middle Eastern and Indian sweets. As it has a lengthy history of use in European baking and *pâtisserie*, it may be found in many good food shops.

SILVER LEAF *Varg*

These sheets of edible thinly beaten silver leaf are used to decorate special-occasion dishes for festivals and family events. They can usually be bought in better Indian and Pakistani shops.

Starters and Snacks

PRAWN AND VEGETABLE KEBABS

These 'kebabs' are coated with breadcrumbs and may be grilled or lightly fried. They may either be served with a salad as a starter or as one of the dishes of the main meal.

SERVES 4
(MAKES 10-12)

PREPARATION
about 30 minutes
COOKING
about 25 minutes

Calories per serving *340*
Total fat *Low*
Saturated fat *Low*
Protein *Medium*
Carbohydrate *High*
Cholesterol per serving
88 mg
Vitamins *A, B group, C, E*
Minerals *Calcium,
Potassium, Iron, Zinc,
Iodine*

125 g / 4½ oz peeled cooked prawns
2 potatoes
2 carrots
60 g / 2 oz green beans
60 g / 2 oz petits pois
60 g / 2 oz sweetcorn kernels
1 tablespoon lemon juice
2 tablespoons crushed dried red chillies

1 large garlic clove, crushed
2.5-cm / 1-inch piece of ginger, shredded
1 tablespoon chopped fresh coriander, plus more whole leaves to garnish
salt
175 g / 6 oz breadcrumbs
2 tablespoons corn oil

1 Coarsely chop the prawns. Peel the potatoes and cook them whole in boiling salted water until just tender. Drain and allow to cool slightly, then mash lightly with a fork or potato masher and set aside.

2 Peel the carrots and cut them into very fine batons about 1 cm / ½ inch long. Cut the green beans into similar lengths.

3 In a pan of boiling salted water, blanch the green beans, peas and sweetcorn for 2 minutes. Drain and set aside.

4 Place all these vegetables and the pieces of prawn in a large bowl. Using a fork, mix everything together. Add the lemon juice, the crushed dried chillies, the garlic, the ginger and the fresh coriander. Season with salt to taste.

5 Once everything is well blended, break off small balls and mould them into round flat shapes in the palms of your hands (the mixture should be sufficient to make 10-12). Dip these into the breadcrumbs and place them on a tray.

6 Heat half the oil in a large non-stick frying pan. Carefully drop half the kebabs into the frying pan

and press them down with a spatula. Cook over a moderate heat for 1-2 minutes on each side, until golden brown. Remove, drain briefly on paper towels and place on a warmed serving dish. Keep warm while you cook the rest of the kebabs in the remaining oil in the same way. Serve garnished with some whole coriander leaves.

Previous pages: Prawn and Vegetable Kebabs served with a mixed herb salad and Quick Mint and Cucumber Raita (page 145)

POTATO KEBABS WITH MINCED PRAWN FILLING

In India and Pakistan, what might be called here 'cakes' or croquettes are referred to as kabab, *and the term 'cake' is almost entirely limited to sweets. These potato kebabs make a delicious starter, served with Date and Tamarind Chutney (page 140) and a raita. If you wish to grill the kebabs, omit the egg and just lightly brush the kebabs with some oil before grilling them on both sides.*

4-5 medium-sized potatoes
2 tablespoons chopped fresh coriander leaves
1 tablespoon chopped fresh mint
1-2 fresh red chillies, chopped
salt

for the filling:
175 g / 6 oz peeled cooked prawns
8 mushrooms, diced

½ teaspoon ginger pulp (page 17)
½ teaspoon garlic pulp (page 17)
½ teaspoon chilli powder
1 tablespoon chopped fresh coriander
1 teaspoon lemon juice
salt
about 1 tablespoon corn oil
1 large egg, beaten

SERVES 4
(MAKES 8-10)

PREPARATION
*about 30 minutes,
plus cooling*
COOKING
about 20-25 minutes

Calories per serving *211*
Total fat *Low*
Saturated fat *Low*
Protein *High*
Carbohydrate *Medium*
Cholesterol per serving
184 mg
Vitamins *A, B group, C, E*
Minerals *Potassium, Iron,
Zinc, Selenium, Iodine*

1 Peel the potatoes and cut them into chunks. Boil them in plenty of salted water until tender, then drain and mash them.

2 While the mashed potatoes are still warm, add to them the fresh coriander, mint, red chillies and salt to taste. Leave to cool at room temperature.

3 Now make the filling: chop the prawns to a coarse mince. Place in a small heavy-based saucepan. Add the mushrooms, followed by the ginger, garlic, chilli, coriander, lemon juice and salt to taste.

4 Place over a moderate heat and cook the filling for 2-3 minutes, stirring continuously. Once all the liquid has evaporated, remove the pan from the heat and transfer its contents to a plate to cool.

5 Now take the mashed potato mixture and break off 8-10 small balls of it a little larger than a golf ball. Mould each into a flat round shape in the palm of your hand. Make a dimple in the middle and fill this with the prawn and mushroom filling (about a level teaspoon). Fold the potato over the filling and again flatten it into a round shape.

6 When all the kebabs are ready, pour about 1 tablespoon of corn oil into a non-stick frying pan and place over a moderate heat. Dip each kebab in the beaten egg and fry, turning at least twice, for 1 or 2 minutes on each side, until golden brown on both sides.

7 When all are ready, serve 2 or 3 per person.

SHALLOT AND KING PRAWN STARTER WITH HONEY AND SCALLOPS

King or tiger prawns are readily available from most good supermarkets. If using fresh prawns, cut off the heads, peel off the shells and use a knife to remove the black vein of intestinal tract along their length. Frozen prawns should be defrosted before cooking. If using ready-cooked prawns, add them with the scallops just to heat them through as the scallops cook. I often serve this delicious starter on a bed of mixed salad leaves, such as lettuce, endive, radish and fresh coriander. Add a few slices of red pepper, if you wish, for more texture.

SERVES 4

PREPARATION

about 10-15 minutes
COOKING
about 10 minutes

Calories per serving *107*
Total fat *Low*
Saturated fat *Low*
Protein *High*
Carbohydrate *Low*
Cholesterol per serving
82 mg
Vitamins *B₃, B₁₂*
Minerals *Potassium, Zinc,
Selenium, Iodine*

8 king prawns, fresh or frozen peeled and cooked
8 scallops
2 tablespoons ginger and garlic sauce (see page 17)
3 tablespoons clear honey

½ teaspoon salt
2 shallots, finely chopped
1 green chilli, finely chopped
lime wedges to serve

1   Peel and de-vein the fresh prawns as above or, if you are using frozen, allow them to defrost completely. Drain and pat them dry with paper towels. Do the same with the scallops if frozen.

2   In a kadahi, wok or deep frying pan, mix the ginger and garlic sauce with the honey, salt and 150 ml / ¼ pint water. Bring to the boil.

3   Reduce the heat to very low and add the shallots and chilli. Cook for a minute or so, then add the prawns and gently stir-fry for 1-2 minutes. Add the scallops and stir-fry for 1-2 minutes more, until the prawns and scallops are just firm when pressed. (Never overcook prawns or scallops.)

4   Serve warm, with wedges of lime.

Shallot and King Prawn Starter with Honey and Scallops

CHOHLAY
Chickpea Snack

This sweet-and-sour treat is one of the most popular snacks all over the Indian subcontinent. It may be eaten at any time of the day and makes an excellent accompaniment to almost any meal. I recommend using canned chickpeas as they have just the right texture for the dish.

SERVES 4

PREPARATION
about 20 minutes
COOKING
about 10 minutes

Calories per serving *354*
Total fat *Low*
Saturated fat *Low*
Protein *High*
Carbohydrate *Low*
Cholesterol per serving
None
Vitamins $B_1, B_3, B_6,$
Folate, C, E
Minerals *Calcium,*
Potassium, Iron, Zinc

two 450-g / 1-lb cans of chickpeas
1 large potato, cubed
1 medium onion, diced
2 tablespoons tamarind paste
1 teaspoon mango powder
1 teaspoon garam masala
1 teaspoon ground coriander
½ teaspoon ground ginger
1 teaspoon chilli powder

2 tablespoons tomato ketchup
2 tablespoons sugar
salt
1 tablespoon chopped fresh mint
2 tablespoons fresh coriander
4 baby tomatoes, sliced
3 baby onions, sliced
1 red chilli
1 green chilli

1 Drain the chickpeas well and place them in a large serving bowl.

2 Boil the potato and onion until soft but not mushy. Drain and set aside.

3 In a large bowl, blend together the tamarind, mango powder, garam masala, ground coriander, ginger, chilli powder, tomato ketchup, sugar and salt to taste, with 150 ml / ¼ pint water. Pour this sweet-and-sour sauce over the top of the chickpeas. Add the potatoes and onions to this and mix everything together gently.

4 Mix in half the fresh mint and half the fresh coriander and garnish with the remaining mint and coriander and the tomatoes and onions. Arrange the two chillies crossed on top and serve.

MASALA PRAWN AND VEGETABLE SAMOSAS

These adaptations of traditional samosas substitute filo pastry for the usual more stodgy wrapping, and they are baked rather than deep-fried. As well as making an interesting and unusual starter, they can be served with drinks or as a snack at any time of the day.

12 sheets of filo pastry
2 tablespoons groundnut oil
175 g / 6 oz peeled cooked prawns
1 tablespoon tomato purée
1 teaspoon garam masala
1 teaspoon chilli powder
½ teaspoon ground coriander
1 teaspoon garlic pulp (page 17)
1 teaspoon ginger pulp (page 17)

salt
4 tablespoons virtually fat-free fromage frais
1 tablespoon chopped fresh coriander leaves
2 teaspoons lemon juice
4 mushrooms, thinly sliced
½ red pepper, deseeded and diced
1 carrot, diced
60 g / 2 oz sweetcorn kernels

SERVES 4
(MAKES 8)

PREPARATION
about 15 minutes
COOKING
15-20 minutes

Calories per samosa *44*
Total fat *Medium*
Saturated fat *Low*
Protein *High*
Carbohydrate *High*
Cholesterol per serving
21 mg
Vitamins *A, B₁₂*
Minerals *Iodine, Selenium,*
Potassium

1   Preheat the oven to 190°C/375°F/gas 5. Keep the sheets of pastry rolled together under a damp cloth as otherwise they dry out fast and become difficult to work with. Rinse the prawns and pat them dry with paper towels.

2   In a bowl, mix together the tomato purée, garam masala, chilli powder, ground coriander, garlic, ginger, salt, fromage frais, fresh coriander and lemon juice, together with 4 tablespoons water.

3   Transfer this mixture to a kadahi, wok or deep frying pan and cook over a moderate heat for about 1 minute.

4   Add the prawns, mushrooms, pepper, carrot and sweetcorn. Stir-fry over a medium to low heat for 5-7 minutes, or until the mixture has become fairly dry. Remove the mixture from the heat.

5   Working quickly with 2 or 3 sheets of pastry at a time and using a plate or saucer as a template, cut two or three 15-cm / 5-inch rounds from each sheet. Oil each round lightly and arrange 3 rounds on top of each other. Put about one-eighth of the prawn and vegetable mixture just to one side of the centre of the the pastry round and fold the pastry over to make a semi-circle. Press down lightly and seal by folding the edges two or three times like a hem and pinching. Brush the outside of the parcel lightly with oil.

6   Once all the samosas are made, put them in the oven and bake for about 25 minutes until just nicely golden.

MASALA GRILLED COD STEAKS WITH TOMATO

These spicy cod steaks make a very attractive starter, accompanied by the mixed salad suggested below. They may also be served as one of several main-course dishes.

SERVES 4

PREPARATION
*about 25 minutes,
plus 30 minutes'
marinating*
COOKING
8-12 minutes

Calories per serving 180
Total fat *Low*
Saturated fat *Low*
Protein *High*
Carbohydrate *Low*
Cholesterol per serving
58 mg
Vitamins *A, B group, C, E*
Minerals *Iron, Selenium,
Iodine, Potassium*

4 cod steaks, each about 125 g / 4½ oz
1 tablespoon sunflower oil
3 tablespoons lemon juice
1 teaspoon garlic pulp (page 17)
1 teaspoon crushed dried red chillies
*1 tablespoon chopped fresh coriander leaves,
plus 4 sprigs for garnish*
1 large fresh red chilli, finely chopped
salt
2 firm tomatoes, chopped

1 teaspoon shredded ginger pieces
1 lime, quartered, to serve

for the mixed salad:
3 leaves from an iceberg lettuce, torn into strips
8-10 whole baby spinach leaves
1 red onion, sliced into rings
½ cucumber, thinly sliced
2 carrots, finely grated
1 tablespoon lemon juice

1 Rinse the cod steaks and pat them dry. Place them in a heatproof dish.

2 In a bowl, mix together the oil, lemon juice, garlic, crushed chillies, chopped coriander, fresh red chilli and salt to taste. Using a pastry brush, spread this mixture all over the cod steaks and set aside for about half an hour.

3 When ready to cook, heat the grill until it is as hot as you can get it, then turn it down to moderate. Place the cod steaks under it and grill them for about 7-10 minutes, or until the cod is cooked right through (the flesh flakes readily when pushed with a fork). Remove the steaks from under the grill and baste with any juices that have formed around the fish.

4 Sprinkle the tomato and shredded ginger over the fish steaks. Return to the grill and cook for a further 1-2 minutes.

5 Meanwhile, mix the leaves, onion, cucumber and carrot in a large bowl for the salad.

6 Remove the fish from the grill, arrange on 4 individual plates and garnish with the coriander sprigs. Arrange the salad beside the cod steaks, sprinkle with lemon juice and, if you wish, a little salt. Serve with a lime quarter on each plate.

Masala Grilled Cod Steaks with Tomato

AVOCADO WITH SPICY LEMON PRAWNS

Though avocado is not an Indian fruit, it is one of my favourites and the spicy prawn dressing makes this version of a traditional starter taste very special.

SERVES 4

PREPARATION
about 20 minutes

Calories per serving *243*
Total fat *High*
Saturated fat *Medium*
Protein *Medium*
Carbohydrate *Low*
Cholesterol per serving
92 mg
Vitamins *B group, C, E*
Minerals *Potassium, Iron,
Zinc, Iodine*

2 avocados
zest and 3 tablespoons juice from 1 lemon
125 g / 4½ oz peeled cooked prawns
5 tablespoons low-fat mayonnaise
1 teaspoon crushed coriander seeds
1 teaspoon crushed dried red chillies
2 tablespoons chopped fresh coriander leaves

1 fresh green chilli, chopped
1 fresh red chilli, chopped

for the garnish:
1 tablespoon sesame seeds
4 sprigs of fresh coriander

1 Halve the avocados and remove the stones. Brush the exposed flesh with a little of the lemon juice to prevent discoloration. Place the avocados cut side down on serving plates.
2 Squeeze out any excess water from the prawns.
3 Mix together the mayonnaise, lemon zest and juice, coriander seeds, dried chillies, fresh coriander, and fresh green and red chillies. Add the prawns and blend everything together.
4 Turn the avocado halves over and spoon equal amounts of the mixture into them. Serve garnished with the sesame seeds and fresh coriander sprigs.

TROUT-FILLED BEEF TOMATOES

SERVES 4

PREPARATION
about 20 minutes
COOKING
25-30 minutes

Calories per serving *182*
Total fat *High*
Saturated fat *Low*
Protein *High*
Carbohydrate *Low*
Cholesterol per serving
55 mg
Vitamins *A, B group, C, E*
Minerals *Potassium, Iron,
Zinc, Selenium, Iodine*

4 large beef tomatoes
3 small trout fillets
2 tablespoons olive oil
1 onion, thinly sliced
large pinch of onion seeds
4 curry leaves

2 garlic cloves, halved lengthwise
1 teaspoon shredded ginger
60 g / 2 oz fresh or frozen peas
1 tablespoon chopped fresh coriander leaves
2 red chillies, sliced
salt

1 Cut the tops off the tomatoes and, using a grapefruit knife, remove the flesh (use for a sauce or another dish). Cut the trout fillets into small bite-sized pieces. Preheat a moderate grill.
2 Heat the olive oil in a kadahi, wok or deep frying pan and fry the onion, onion seeds, curry leaves, garlic and ginger for about 30 seconds.
3 Drop in the pieces of trout and stir-fry for about 5 minutes, trying not to break up the pieces.
4 Throw in the peas and the fresh coriander. Cook for a further 3-5 minutes. Finally add the red chillies and mix in well. Season the mixture to taste with salt and use to stuff the tomatoes.
5 Place the tomatoes under the grill for 10-15 minutes, until they begin to brown on top.

CHICKEN LIVERS WITH SPRING ONION

Chicken livers used not to be very popular in India and Pakistan. Probably because they are so tasty and economical, however, recently more and more people on the subcontinent have started to enjoy them and eat them quite regularly. Serve them with a salad or on a bed of leaves, and with some naan *(page 124).*

450 g / 1 lb chicken livers
½ teaspoon turmeric
salt
2 tablespoons corn oil
3 whole garlic cloves
1 teaspoon shredded ginger

6 curry leaves
2 green chillies, sliced lengthwise
bunch of spring onions, sliced thickly at an angle
1 teaspoon lemon juice
1 tablespoon chopped fresh coriander

SERVES 4

PREPARATION
about 25 minutes
COOKING
about 10 minutes

1 Trim the chicken livers well, removing any fatty tubes or any darkened or discoloured edges. Rub the livers with a mixture of about ½ teaspoon of turmeric and ½ teaspoon of salt and then rinse to remove any lingering odours. Set the livers aside on paper towel to drain.

2 Heat the oil in a kadahi, wok or deep frying pan over a moderate heat and stir-fry the garlic, ginger and curry leaves for about 30 seconds.

3 Add the chicken livers, followed by the green chillies and salt to taste, and stir-fry for 5-7 minutes. Throw in the spring onions and sprinkle in the lemon juice, followed by the fresh coriander. Cook for about a minute more.

4 Transfer to a warmed serving dish and serve immediately.

Calories per serving *162*
Total fat *High*
Saturated fat *Low*
Protein *High*
Carbohydrate *Low*
Cholesterol per serving
428 g
Vitamins *A, B group, C, E*
Minerals *Potassium, Iron, Zinc*

GRILLED CHICKEN BOTI KEBABS

Boti simply means 'pieces of meat'. These kebabs go well with the Tomato and Onion Raita on page 142. Served with some naan *(page 124), they can also make a good light lunch. For a sweet-and-sour flavour to the marinade, omit the mint and garam masala and replace them with 2 tablespoons of tamarind paste and 3 tablespoons each of tomato ketchup and clear honey.*

SERVES 4

PREPARATION
*about 25 minutes,
plus 30 minutes'
marinating*
COOKING
about 10 minutes

Calories per serving *164*
Total fat *Medium*
Saturated fat *Low*
Protein *High*
Carbohydrate *Low*
Cholesterol per serving
50 mg
Vitamins *A, B group, C, E*
Minerals *Calcium,
Potassium, Iron, Zinc,
Iodine*

275 g / 10 oz boned skinless chicken portions
175 ml / 6 fl oz plain low-fat runny yoghurt
1 teaspoon garam masala
1 teaspoon ground coriander
1 teaspoon ginger pulp (page 17)
1 teaspoon mint sauce
2 garlic cloves, finely chopped
½ teaspoon chilli powder
1 tablespoon chopped fresh coriander leaves
2 fresh red chillies, chopped

1 teaspoon salt
8-10 whole shallots
1 courgette, thickly sliced
8-10 cherry tomatoes
1 large green pepper, deseeded and cut into chunks
1 tablespoon corn oil
1 tablespoon lemon juice
1 onion, halved and thinly sliced, for garnish
few spinach or lettuce leaves, shredded, for garnish

1 Cut the chicken into bite-sized cubes and put them in a deep bowl.

2 Put the yoghurt in a food processor and add the garam masala, ground coriander, ginger, mint sauce, garlic, chilli powder, fresh coriander and 1 of the chopped red chillies with salt to taste. Whisk everything together for about 30 seconds. Pour this over the chicken, mix well and leave to marinate for about half an hour. Prepare the vegetables and stir them into the marinade as they are ready.

3 Preheat a moderate grill. Add the oil to the marinade and mix everything together well.

4 Arrange the chicken and vegetable pieces on skewers and grill for 7-10 minutes, turning the skewers from time to time and brushing with the marinade, until the chicken is cooked through and scorch marks begin to appear on top of the chicken and vegetables.

5 Serve sprinkled with the lemon juice and garnished with the onion, shredded leaves and chilli.

Grilled Chicken Boti Kebabs served with Naan (page 124)

MUSHROOM AND FRESH CORIANDER SOUP

SERVES 4

PREPARATION
15-20 minutes
COOKING
about 20-25 minutes

Calories per serving *125*
Total fat *High*
Saturated fat *Medium*
Protein *High*
Carbohydrate *Low*
Cholesterol per serving
9 mg
Vitamins *B group, C, E*
Minerals *Calcium,*
Potassium, Zinc, Iodine,
Selenium

1 small onion
350 g / 12 oz mushrooms
2 tablespoons olive oil
1 whole bay leaf
salt
½ teaspoon coarsely ground pepper
30 g / 1 oz ground almonds

¼ teaspoon freshly grated nutmeg
450 ml / ¾ pint semi-skimmed milk
1 tablespoon chopped fresh coriander leaves, plus more for garnish
1 tablespoon virtually fat-free fromage frais
paprika for garnish

1 Dice the onion, wipe the mushrooms clean with a damp cloth and slice coarsely.

2 Heat the oil in a heavy-based saucepan, add the onion and bay leaf and cook for 1½ minutes. Add the mushrooms and cook, stirring, for 3-5 minutes.

3 Lower the heat slightly and add salt to taste, the pepper, ground almonds and nutmeg. Stir in 300 ml / ½ pint water and the milk. Bring back to just below the boil, cover with a lid and simmer gently for 7-10 minutes, stirring from time to time.

4 Add the fresh coriander, carefully transfer the soup to a liquidizer or food processor (in batches if necessary) and process until smooth.

5 Return the soup to the pan and reheat. Stir in the fromage frais and serve, garnished with more chopped fresh coriander and a sprinkle of paprika.

LEEK AND POTATO SOUP WITH CORIANDER

SERVES 4

PREPARATION
about 25 minutes
COOKING
about 30 minutes

Calories per serving *421*
Total fat *High*
Saturated fat *High*
Protein *Low*
Carbohydrate *Low*
Cholesterol per serving
21 mg
Vitamins *A, B group, C, E*
Minerals *Calcium,*
Potassium, Iron, Zinc,
Iodine

3 leeks, trimmed and coarsely chopped
3 medium-sized potatoes, coarsely diced
1 celery stalk, trimmed and coarsely chopped
1 medium-sized carrot, coarsely chopped
2 tablespoons corn oil
600 ml / 1 pint semi-skimmed milk
½ teaspoon garlic pulp (page 17)

½ teaspoon garam masala
salt
150 ml / ¼ pint low-fat crème fraîche
175 g / 6 oz virtually fat-free fromage frais
2 tablespoons chopped fresh coriander leaves, to garnish

1 In a heavy-based saucepan over a moderate heat, fry all the vegetables in the oil, stirring occasionally, for about 3-5 minutes.

2 Add 600 ml / 1 pint of water, the milk, garlic, salt and garam masala. Bring to the boil and simmer until half has evaporated, 15-20 minutes.

3 Remove from the heat, allow to cool slightly and stir in the crème fraîche and fromage frais. Carefully transfer to a blender or food processor and purée the soup (in batches if necessary). Adjust the seasoning.

4 Return soup to the pan and bring back to just below the boil. Serve garnished with the coriander.

Mushroom and Fresh Coriander Soup served with Naan (page 124)

Fish and Shellfish

PLAICE FILLETS WITH A FENUGREEK SAUCE

Fenugreek, whether fresh or dried, has a beautiful fragrance. I have used both powdered and fresh for this sauce and I am sure you will agree that it produces a wonderful result. Serve the fish with Aromatic Rice with Peas (page 126) or plain boiled rice.

SERVES 4

PREPARATION
10 minutes
COOKING
about 20 minutes

Calories per serving *141*
Total fat *Medium*
Saturated fat *Medium*
Protein *High*
Carbohydrate *None*
Cholesterol per serving
63 mg
Vitamins *B group*
Minerals *Selenium, Iodine, Potassium*

4 large skinless plaice fillets
2 tablespoons low-fat crème fraîche
¼ teaspoon turmeric
1 teaspoon garlic pulp (page 17)
1 teaspoon crushed dried red chillies
large pinch of ground fenugreek
1 teaspoon ground coriander

salt
2 tablespoons olive oil
large pinch of mustard seeds
6 curry leaves
1 tablespoon fresh fenugreek leaves
6-8 cherry tomatoes
1 fresh green chilli, cut lengthwise

1 Preheat the oven to 190°C/375°F/gas 5. Wash the plaice fillets, pat them dry and place them in a heatproof dish.

2 Pour the crème fraîche into a mixing bowl and add the turmeric, garlic, dried chillies, ground fenugreek, ground coriander, salt to taste and 300 ml / ½ pint water. Whisk everything together well.

3 In a frying pan, heat the oil over a medium heat and throw in the mustard seeds and curry leaves. Wait about 20 seconds and remove from the heat.

4 Add the crème fraîche sauce to the pan. Using a whisk, mix it in fully and return to the heat. Cook over a low heat for 3-5 minutes.

5 Add the fenugreek leaves and pour the sauce over the fillets. Place the fillets in the oven and cook for 7-10 minutes. Check that the fillets are cooked (the flesh flakes when pushed with a fork).

6 Garnish with the cherry tomatoes and the chilli strips to serve.

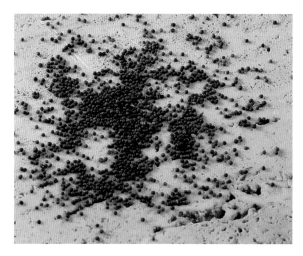

Previous pages: Barbecued Marinated Seafood served with plain boiled basmati rice

LEMON AND GARLIC PLAICE

Plaice grills well and, lightly flavoured with lemon and garlic, it goes nicely with Rice with Pine Nuts (page 128).

4 large skinless plaice fillets
2 tablespoons olive oil
3 spring onions, finely chopped
1 green chilli, deseeded and diced
1 red chilli, deseeded and diced

2 tablespoons chopped fresh coriander leaves
2 garlic cloves, crushed
pinch of salt
3 tablespoons lemon juice

1 Rinse the plaice fillets, pat them dry and put them in a heatproof dish.

2 In a bowl, mix together the oil, spring onions, chillies, fresh coriander and garlic. Finally add the salt and lemon juice and set aside.

3 Preheat a moderate grill. Pour the dressing over the plaice and grill for 10-15 minutes, turning halfway through and basting from time to time.

SERVES 4

PREPARATION
about 20 minutes
COOKING
10-15 minutes

Calories per serving *190*
Total fat *Medium*
Saturated fat *Low*
Protein *High*
Carbohydrate *Low*
Cholesterol per serving
79 mg
Vitamins *B group, C*
Minerals *Selenium, Iodine, Potassium*

BARBECUED MARINATED SEAFOOD

I have selected some of my favourite seafood to barbecue, but you could choose different fish. For fuller flavours it is always better to marinate the pieces to be grilled overnight. Serve with rice (see page 46).

15 peeled cooked king prawns
2-3 skinless plaice fillets
2-3 skinless cod fillets
3 skinless trout fillets
sliced red onion and coriander sprigs, for garnish
lime or lemon slices, to serve

for the marinade :
2 tablespoons tomato purée
125 ml / 4 fl oz plain low-fat runny yoghurt

1 teaspoon ginger pulp (page 17)
1 teaspoon garlic pulp (page 17)
1 teaspoon chilli powder
½ teaspoon turmeric
1½ teaspoons ground coriander
1 teaspoon ground cumin
1 tablespoon chopped fresh coriander leaves
1 tablespoon corn oil
2 tablespoons lemon juice
salt

1 First make the marinade: in a large bowl, blend together all the ingredients with salt to taste.

2 Rinse the prawns and fish and pat dry. Cut the fish into bite-sized cubes. Place the pieces of fish and the prawns in the marinade, mix well and leave in the refrigerator, covered, either overnight or for at least 3 hours, stirring from time to time.

3 Prepare the barbecue well ahead to get it really hot. When ready to cook, remove the fish from the marinade and barbecue the pieces of fish and the prawns a few at a time, getting them nice and brown all over. Eat them as they come off the barbecue, accompanied by slices of lime or lemon and garnished with red onion and coriander.

SERVES 4

PREPARATION
20 minutes, plus at least 3 hours' marinating
COOKING
15-20 minutes

Calories per serving *295*
Total fat *Medium*
Saturated fat *Low*
Protein *High*
Carbohydrate *Low*
Cholesterol per serving
245 mg
Vitamins *A, B group, E*
Minerals *Calcium, Potassium, Iron, Zinc, Selenium, Iodine*

COD WITH MUSHROOMS AND GREEN CHILLIES

Green chillies are lightly fried in the oil, drained and added to the cod at the end to give this dish a beautiful aroma and flavour. Serve it with freshly cooked chapati *(see page 124).*

SERVES 4

PREPARATION
about 20 minutes
COOKING
10-15 minutes

Calories per serving *149*
Total fat *High*
Saturated fat *Low*
Protein *High*
Carbohydrate *Low*
Cholesterol per serving
27 mg
Vitamins *B group, C, E*
Minerals *Potassium,
Selenium, Iodine*

275 g / 10 oz skinless pieces of cod, coarsely cubed
2-3 tablespoons corn oil
5 green chillies, slit down one side and deseeded
6 curry leaves
large pinch of onion seeds
large pinch of mustard seeds
2 onions, sliced
1 teaspoon ginger pulp (page 17)
1 teaspoon garlic pulp (page 17)
1 level teaspoon chilli powder
salt
1 tablespoon lemon juice
115 g / 4 oz mushrooms, sliced
1 tablespoon chopped fresh coriander leaves, plus more whole leaves for garnish

1   When you have prepared the cod by rinsing it and patting it dry, leave it in the refrigerator so the pieces stay firm.

2   Heat the oil in a kadahi, wok or deep frying pan and fry the green chillies for about 1 minute. Remove them from the pan, draining off as much oil as possible, and drain further on paper towels.

3   Gently stir-fry the pieces of cod over a moderate heat for about 1½ minutes and carefully remove from the pan. Keep warm.

4   In the remaining oil over a moderate heat, fry the curry leaves, onion and mustard seeds and the sliced onions for 2-3 minutes, stirring occasionally.

5   Pour in the ginger, garlic, chilli powder, salt and lemon juice, followed by the mushrooms. Stir to mix everything together. Return to the pan the cod and the fried green chillies, followed by the chopped coriander. Mix again gently. Lower the heat, cover the pan and cook gently for 5-7 minutes, checking occasionally to make sure the mixture doesn't catch.

6   Serve garnished with whole coriander leaves.

Cod with Mushrooms and Green Chillies

PLAICE FILLETS WITH A CREAMY CORIANDER TOPPING

Serve this dish with a salad of red onion, rocket and basil or Cauliflower with Peppers (page 117).

SERVES 4

PREPARATION
10 minutes
COOKING
about 10 minutes

Calories per serving *200*
Total fat *Medium*
Saturated fat *Low*
Protein *High*
Carbohydrate *Low*
Cholesterol per serving
92 mg
Vitamins *B group*
Minerals *Potassium, Zinc,
Selenium, Iodine*

4 large skinless plaice fillets
3 tablespoons half-fat fromage frais
1 green chilli, chopped
2 tablespoons chopped fresh coriander leaves
2 tablespoons lime juice

large pinch of salt
1 teaspoon sesame seeds
1 tablespoon corn oil
1 red chilli, chopped , for garnish
lime wedges, to serve

1   Rinse the fillets, pat them dry and put them in a heatproof dish.

2   Mix together the fromage frais, chilli, coriander, lime juice and salt and whisk well. Add the sesame seeds and corn oil to the creamy sauce.

3   Preheat a moderate grill. Using a pastry brush, brush the sauce over the fish fillets and place them under the grill for 7-10 minutes, or until cooked through. Turn once halfway through. Serve with lime wedges and garnished with chopped red chilli.

COD FILLETS WITH SPICY GRAM FLOUR COATING

This deliciously spicy fish dish is good served with a dhal and rice.

SERVES 4

PREPARATION
about 15 minutes
COOKING
about 10 minutes

Calories per serving *241*
Total fat *Medium*
Saturated fat *Low*
Protein *High*
Carbohydrate *Low*
Cholesterol per serving
78 mg
Vitamins *A, B group, C, E*
Minerals *Potassium, Iron,
Selenium, Iodine*

4 large skinless cod fillets
2 tablespoons gram flour (page 29)
1 tablespoon plain flour
1 tablespoon mango powder (page 10)
1 teaspoon chilli powder
1 teaspoon ground ginger

1 teaspoon garlic powder
pinch of salt
2 teaspoons crushed coriander seeds
2 tablespoons corn oil
lemon wedges, to serve

1   Rinse the cod fillets and pat them dry. Leave them in the refrigerator to firm up.

2   Mix together the gram flour with the plain flour, mango powder, chilli powder, ginger, garlic powder, salt and the crushed coriander seeds.

3   Remove the fillets from the refrigerator and dust them with the flour mixture. Set aside.

4   Heat half the oil in a large non-stick frying pan and gently drop in 2 of the fillets. Lower the heat and cook for 2-3 minutes each side, turning twice to ensure even cooking, until cooked through.

5   Transfer the cooked fillets to a warmed serving platter and cook the remaining fillets in the same way. Serve with lemon wedges.

Plaice Fillets with a Creamy Coriander Topping

MONKFISH WITH GARLIC

Monkfish is a good fish to use for stir-frying as it does not break up easily. This dish, which includes carrots and parsnips (see page 56), is delicious served with chapati *(see page 124) and a wet dish like a* dhal.

SERVES 4

PREPARATION
about 20 minutes
COOKING
20-25 minutes

Calories per serving *191*
Total fat *Medium*
Saturated fat *Low*
Protein *High*
Carbohydrate *Low*
Cholesterol per serving
10 mg
Vitamins *A B group, C, E*
Minerals *Potassium, Iron,*
Selenium, Iodine

275 g / 10 oz monkfish fillet
2 tablespoons olive oil
1 bay leaf
3 garlic cloves
1 large leek, sliced
6 black peppercorns, crushed
1 teaspoon crushed dried red chillies

large pinch of salt
2 carrots, cut into batons
2 parsnips, cut into batons
1 tablespoon chopped fresh mint
1 tablespoon chopped fresh coriander leaves
2 red chillies, sliced
more whole coriander and mint leaves, for garnish

1   Prepare the monkfish by cutting it into cubes and set aside.

2   Heat the olive oil in a kadahi, wok or deep frying pan over a moderate heat and add the bay leaf, garlic cloves, leek, peppercorns and dried chillies. Cook for 2-3 minutes, stirring occasionally.

3   Add the salt, followed by the carrots and parsnips. Cook over a low heat for a further 2-3 minutes, stirring occasionally. Remove from the heat, add the monkfish and mix it in well before returning the pan to the heat and continuing to stir-fry for 5-7 minutes.

4   Add the mint, the chopped coriander and sliced fresh chillies. Cover and cook on the lowest possible heat for 5-7 minutes.

5   Serve immediately, garnished with more whole mint and coriander leaves.

TROUT WITH BABY POTATOES AND CAULIFLOWER

Potatoes and cauliflower complement each other beautifully and are both extremely versatile, as much at home with fish and seafood as with meat and poultry. Serve this dish with chapati *(see page 124).*

SERVES 4

PREPARATION
about 25 minutes
COOKING
20-25 minutes

Calories per serving *238*
Total fat *Medium*
Saturated fat *Low*
Protein *High*
Carbohydrate *Low*
Cholesterol per serving
None
Vitamins *B group, C, E*
Minerals *Potassium, Iron,*
Zinc, Selenium

275 g / 10 oz skinless trout fillets
8-10 baby potatoes
salt
2 tablespoons corn oil
2 medium onions sliced
¼ teaspoon mixed onion and mustard seeds
6 curry leaves

½ small cauliflower, separated into florets
3 garlic cloves
½ teaspoon ginger pulp (page 17)
1 teaspoon crushed dried red chillies
2 green chillies, sliced
1 tablespoon chopped fresh coriander leaves
1 tablespoon lemon juice

1   Cut the trout fillets across into thick slices and set aside.

2   Scrub the potatoes lightly and halve them. Boil them in salted water for about 15 minutes or until

they are just tender. Drain well.

3 Heat the oil in a kadahi, wok or deep frying pan and fry the onions, mixed seeds and curry leaves for about 2 minutes.

4 Add to the pan the cauliflower florets and the potatoes, together with the whole garlic cloves, ginger, dried red chillies and the trout. Stir-fry for about 2 minutes, stirring gently to avoid breaking up any of the ingredients.

5 Add the fresh green chillies, coriander and the lemon juice. Cover and cook over a low heat for 1 minute before serving.

BAKED TROUT WITH SPICY ALMOND AND COCONUT SAUCE

I am pleased to say that good-quality ready-prepared trout is widely available from our supermarkets, making this rich variation on a classic European dish very quick indeed. Serve it with a simple rice dish.

2 large whole trout, gutted
2 tablespoons lemon juice
2 tablespoons tomato purée
1 tablespoon ground almonds
1 teaspoon ginger pulp (page 17)
1 teaspoon Tabasco sauce
1 teaspoon garlic pulp (page 17)
1 teaspoon garam masala
3 tablespoons low-fat plain runny yoghurt
salt
125 ml / 4 fl oz coconut milk

1 tablespoon chopped fresh coriander leaves
2 tablespoons corn oil
1 small bay leaf
2 black cardamoms
3.5-cm / 1½-inch piece of cinnamon stick

for the garnish:
few flaked almonds
lemon wedges
fresh bay leaves

SERVES 4

PREPARATION
about 15 minutes
COOKING
15-20 minutes

Calories per serving *207*
Total fat *High*
Saturated fat *Low*
Protein *High*
Carbohydrate *Low*
Cholesterol per serving
54 mg
Vitamins *B group, C, E*
Minerals *Potassium, Iron, Selenium, Iodine*

1 Rinse the trout under running water and pat dry with paper towels. Sprinkle the fish with half the lemon juice and place them in an ovenproof dish just big enough to take them in one layer.

2 Preheat the oven to 190°C/375°F/gas 5. In a bowl, mix together the tomato purée, ground almonds, ginger, Tabasco sauce, garlic, garam masala, yoghurt, salt, coconut milk, coriander and the remaining lemon juice. Pour in 125 ml / 4 fl oz of water and blend everything together.

3 In a frying pan, heat the oil with the bay leaf, cardamoms and cinnamon for about 30 seconds. Pour the sauce into this and bring to the boil. Reduce the heat and cook for 1-2 minutes more. Pour this over the trout.

4 Bake in the oven for 10-15 minutes, until cooked through (when pierced with the tip of a knife, the flesh flakes readily).

5 Serve with the garnish.

Overleaf left to right: Monkfish with Garlic, Baked Trout with Spicy Almond and Coconut Sauce

KING PRAWN DOPIAZA WITH MANGO POWDER

SERVES 4

PREPARATION
about 15 minutes
COOKING
20-25 minutes

Calories per serving *149*
Total fat *Medium*
Saturated fat *Low*
Protein *High*
Carbohydrate *Low*
Cholesterol per serving
105 mg
Vitamins *B group, C, E*
Minerals *Potassium, Iron,
Selenium, Iodine*

Dopiaza means simply 'double onions', indicating a dish using masses of them. Try to choose the largest prawns available for this dish, which has a delicious sour tone to it from the mango powder. Serve it with plain boiled rice.

14-16 peeled cooked king prawns
2 tablespoons corn oil
4 onions, thinly sliced
large pinch of onion seeds
4 curry leaves
1 teaspoon garlic pulp (page 17)
1 teaspoon ginger pulp (page 17)

1 teaspoon chilli powder
salt
½ teaspoon turmeric
2 level teaspoons mango powder (page 10)
1 tablespoon chopped fresh coriander leaves
2 green chillies, sliced
2 firm tomatoes, quartered

1 Rinse the prawns and pat dry with paper towels.
2 Heat the oil in a deep frying pan or a heavy-based saucepan over a moderate heat and cook the onions, stirring frequently, until golden brown.
3 Add the onion seeds and curry leaves, and stir-fry for about 2 minutes. Next add the garlic, ginger, chilli powder, salt, turmeric and mango powder and stir-fry for a further 3 minutes.
4 Add the prawns, green chillies, tomatoes and most of the fresh coriander. Lower the heat, cover the pan and cook gently for 5-7 minutes. Serve garnished with the rest of the coriander.

PRAWNS WITH PEAS AND RED PEPPER

SERVES 4

PREPARATION
about 15 minutes
COOKING
15-20 minutes

Calories per serving *169*
Total fat *Medium*
Saturated fat *Low*
Protein *High*
Carbohydrate *Low*
Cholesterol per serving
123 mg
Vitamins *A, B group , C, E*
Minerals *Potassium, Iron,
Zinc, Selenium, Iodine*

175 g / 6 oz peeled cooked prawns
2 tablespoons corn oil
2 onions, diced
1 bay leaf
¼ teaspoon white cumin seeds
2 garlic cloves, sliced in half
1 teaspoon ginger pulp (page 17)

½ teaspoon chilli powder
½ teaspoon ground coriander
salt to taste
175 g / 6 oz freshly podded peas
1 large red pepper, deseeded and coarsely diced
1 tablespoon chopped fresh coriander leaves
juice of ½ lemon

1 Rinse the prawns and pat dry with paper towels.
2 In a kadahi, wok or deep frying pan, heat the oil over a moderate heat and fry the onions with the bay leaf and cumin seeds for about 2 minutes.
3 Add the garlic, ginger, chilli powder, ground coriander and salt. Stir-fry over medium heat for 1 minute. Add the prawns and stir-fry for 4 minutes.
4 Add the peas, red pepper and coriander. Cover and cook for 5-7 minutes, stirring occasionally.
5 Stir in the lemon juice just before serving.

King Prawn Dopiaza with Mango Powder

PASTA WITH PRAWNS AND SUN-DRIED PEPPERS

This dish is fairly quick to prepare and is delicious served with a salad. Try to use small pasta shells or spirals. Sun-dried peppers are becoming increasingly available in supermarkets, delicatessens and health-food shops.

225 g / 8 oz small pasta shells
15 cooked peeled prawns
3 sun-dried peppers
2 tablespoons corn oil
2 garlic cloves, finely chopped
1 tablespoon shredded ginger

4-6 curry leaves
2 spring onions, finely chopped
1 medium courgette, sliced
1 yellow pepper, deseeded and sliced
3 green chillies, diced
1 tablespoon chopped fresh coriander leaves

SERVES 4

PREPARATION
about 20 minutes
COOKING
about 20 minutes

Calories per serving *313*
Total fat *Low*
Saturated fat *Low*
Protein *High*
Carbohydrate *Medium*
Cholesterol per serving
88 mg
Vitamins *A, B group, C, E*
Minerals *Potassium, Iron, Zinc, Selenium, Iodine*

1 Cook the pasta according to packet instructions until just tender, drain and set aside. Stir in a few drops of the oil to prevent the pasta shells from sticking together.

2 Rinse the prawns and then pat them dry with paper towels. Cut the sun-dried peppers into fairly largish slices.

3 Heat the corn oil in a kadahi, wok or deep frying pan over a moderate heat and fry the garlic, ginger and curry leaves. After about 45 seconds, add the chopped spring onions, courgette slices and both the fresh and dried peppers and stir-fry for about 3 minutes.

4 Add the prawns, followed by the green chillies, chopped fresh coriander and the cooked pasta. Stir-fry everything together for a further 2 minutes and serve immediately.

Pasta with Prawns and Sun-Dried Peppers

BALTI TIGER PRAWNS WITH MUSHROOMS

The cuisine of one of the northernmost provinces of Pakistan, Baltistan, brought to the West via the restaurants of Manchester, has recently become very popular. Traditionally cooked in a kadahi, *balti dishes are usually stir-fried and are characterized by their fresh full flavours.*

Frozen shelled tiger prawns are readily available from most good supermarkets. If using fresh, cut off the heads, peel off the shells and use a knife to remove the black vein of intestinal tract along their length. You can use ordinary smaller cooked peeled prawns, but add these later with the mushrooms as they require only very brief cooking.

SERVES 4

PREPARATION
about 15 minutes
COOKING
10-15 minutes

Calories per serving *138*
Total fat *High*
Saturated fat *Low*
Protein *High*
Carbohydrate *Low*
Cholesterol per serving
110 mg
Vitamins *B group, C, E*
Minerals *Potassium, Iron,
Zinc, Selenium, Iodine*

225 g / 8 oz fresh or frozen tiger prawns
175 g / 6 oz mushrooms
2 tablespoons corn oil
2 onions, sliced
½ teaspoon fennel seeds

1 teaspoon crushed dried red chillies
2 garlic cloves, sliced
1 green pepper , deseeded and diced
2 tablespoons chopped fresh coriander

1   If using fresh prawns, peel and de-vein them as described above; if using frozen, allow them to defrost completely, drain any excess liquid and pat the prawns dry with paper towels.

2   Wipe the mushrooms with a damp cloth and slice them thickly.

3   Heat the oil in a kadahi, wok or deep frying pan. Add the sliced onion and the fennel seeds and cook over a fairly high heat until the onions are soft and golden.

4   Add the dried chillies and garlic, followed by the prawns. Cook, stirring occasionally, for 5-7 minutes. Add the mushrooms and green pepper and cook 2-3 minutes more, stirring occasionally.

5   Sprinkle over the fresh coriander to serve.

Balti Tiger Prawns with Mushrooms served with Naan (page 124)

Meat and Poultry

SPICED ROAST POUSSIN

This recipe for baby chickens also works well with other small poultry, such as guinea fowl and quail.

SERVES 4

PREPARATION
about 25 minutes
COOKING
about 45 minutes

Calories per serving *241*
Total fat *High*
Saturated fat *Medium*
Protein *High*
Carbohydrate *Low*
Cholesterol per serving
76 mg
Vitamins *B group, E*
Minerals *Potassium, Iron,*
Zinc, Selenium, Iodine

2 poussins (baby chickens)
1½ tablespoons corn oil
4 shallots, sliced
1 teaspoon garlic pulp (page 17)
1 teaspoon ginger pulp (page 17)
1 teaspoon chilli powder
1 teaspoon ground cumin
1½ teaspoons ground coriander

1 tablespoon ground almonds
salt
¼ teaspoon ground cardamom seeds
3 tablespoons low-fat plain runny yoghurt
1 red onion, chopped, for garnish
1 tomato, chopped, for garnish
1 tablespoon chopped green chilli, for garnish

1 Preheat the oven to 190°C/375°F/gas 5. Wash and pat dry the poussins. Place them on a heatproof dish. Brush inside and out with the oil.

2 Heat the remaining oil in a frying pan and fry the sliced shallots over a moderate heat until soft and golden brown.

3 In a bowl, mix together the garlic, ginger, chilli powder, ground cumin, ground coriander, ground almonds, salt to taste, cardamom and the yoghurt.

Pour this mixture over the onions and quickly stir-fry for about 2 minutes.

4 Remove from the heat, transfer the sauce to a food processor and grind for about 30 seconds or until smooth. Mix in the fresh coriander and mint.

5 Pour the sauce over the chicken and roast in the oven for 30-35 minutes, basting occasionally.

6 Serve the poussins, split into halves or quarters, garnished with red onion, tomato and chilli.

Previous pages: Spiced Roast Poussin served with a Saffron Rice Mould (page 129), Hara Masala Lamb Kebabs (page 94)

BASMATI RICE WITH CHICKEN AND VEGETABLES

Here, basmati rice is cooked with a few fragrant whole spices and then added to a delicious mixture of chicken and vegetables. Accompanied by the refreshing Quick Mint and Cucumber Raita on page 145, this dish makes a complete meal on its own.

2 cups of basmati rice
1 cinnamon stick
2 black cardamom pods
½ teaspoon mixed coloured peppercorns
3 tablespoons chopped fresh coriander leaves
salt
1 tablespoon olive oil
2 tablespoons corn oil
1 onion, sliced
1½ teaspoons ginger pulp (page 17)

1 teaspoon garlic pulp (page 17)
1 teaspoon chilli powder
1½ teaspoons garam masala
1 tablespoon ground almonds
2 tablespoons coconut milk
225 g / 8 oz skinless boned chicken, cut into strips
3 tablespoons lemon juice
60 g / 2 oz peas
60 g / 2 oz sweetcorn kernels
1 red pepper, deseeded and sliced

SERVES 4

PREPARATION
about 25 minutes
COOKING
30-35 minutes

Calories per serving *422*
Total fat *Medium*
Saturated fat *Low*
Protein *Medium*
Carbohydrate *Medium*
Cholesterol per serving
51 mg
Vitamins *B group, C, E*
Minerals *Potassium, Iron, Zinc*

1   Rinse the rice until the water runs clear, and drain it.

2   Place the rice in a saucepan with the cinnamon, cardamoms, peppercorns and 1 tablespoon of the fresh coriander. Add 3 cups of water, salt to taste and the olive oil. Bring to the boil over a high heat. Lower the heat, stir the rice gently and cover with a lid. Cook for 10-15 minutes, until the rice is just tender. Remove from the heat and set aside.

3   In a large kadahi, wok or deep frying pan, heat the oil and fry the onions over moderate heat until golden brown.

4   Reduce the heat and add the ginger, garlic, chilli powder, garam masala, ground almonds, coconut milk and salt to taste. Stir-fry all the ingredients for about 2 minutes.

5   Add the chicken pieces and cook these, stirring occasionally, for 5-7 minutes. Add the lemon juice, followed by the peas, sweetcorn and the red pepper. Stir-fry for a further 2 minutes and finally add another tablespoon of fresh coriander. Add the cooked rice to the pan and gently mix it in.

6   Cover with either a lid or foil and cook over a very low heat for 3-5 minutes before serving, garnished with the remaining fresh coriander.

ROAST CHICKEN
WITH SPICY MUSHROOMS

When roasting, I favour small chickens no bigger than about 1.5 kg / 3¼ lb as they are usually tastier and they are also easier and quicker to cook. Try to choose the best quality virgin olive oil available for this dish, as it will add flavour (and won't smell during cooking).

SERVES 4

PREPARATION
20 minutes
COOKING
*35-40 minutes,
plus 5 minutes'
resting*

Calories per serving *515*
Total fat *High*
Saturated fat *High*
Protein *High*
Carbohydrate *Low*
Cholesterol per serving
206 mg
Vitamins *B group, C, E*
Minerals *Potassium, Iron,
Zinc, Selenium, Iodine*

1 oven-ready chicken, about 1.25-1.5 kg / 2½-3¼ lb
1 tablespoon virgin olive oil
salt
½ teaspoon coarsely ground black pepper

for the spicy mushrooms:
2 tablespoons virgin olive oil
1 onion, finely diced
1 bay leaf

½ teaspoon mixed coloured peppercorns
1 teaspoon ground coriander
large pinch of freshly ground black pepper
large pinch of turmeric
salt
8-10 closed-cap mushrooms, sliced
2 tablespoons chopped fresh coriander leaves
1 red chilli, chopped
2 tablespoons low-fat crème fraîche

1   Preheat the oven to 190°C/375°F/gas 5. Cut the chicken into quarters. Brush all over with olive oil and sprinkle with salt and pepper.

2   Place the chicken in a heatproof dish and roast for 35-40 minutes, basting once or twice.

3   Meanwhile, make the spicy mushrooms: heat the olive oil for 20-30 seconds over a moderate heat. Fry the onion, bay leaf and peppercorns in this for about 2 minutes. Remove from the heat and add the ground coriander, black pepper, turmeric and salt to taste. Return the pan to the heat and fry the spices for a further 30 seconds.

4   Stir in the mushrooms, half the fresh coriander

and the red chilli and stir-fry for another minute. Pour in the crème fraîche, blend it in with all the other ingredients and warm through for about 1 minute. Remove from the heat.

5   Allow the roast chicken to sit in a warm place for about 5 minutes after it comes out of the oven, then cut it into pieces and arrange them on a warmed serving dish (add any juices from the bird to the mushrooms). Remove the skin if you really want to keep the fat and calorie count down. Serve with the mushrooms spooned over the top and garnished with the remaining fresh coriander.

Roast Chicken with Spicy Mushrooms

HALEEM
Cracked Wheat with Strips of Chicken

This dish is traditionally made with lamb. However, this chicken version is perhaps healthier. It is usually served with some trimmings, including ghee, but I suggest using olive oil instead for equally delicious results.

SERVES 4

PREPARATION
*about 25 minutes,
plus overnight
soaking*
COOKING
about 30 minutes

Calories per serving 355
Total fat *Medium*
Saturated fat *Low*
Protein *High*
Carbohydrate *Low*
Cholesterol per serving
64 mg
Vitamins *B group, C , E*
Minerals *Calcium,
Potassium, Iron, Zinc,
Selenium, Iodine*

1 cup of cracked wheat
275 g / 10 oz skinless boned chicken
3 tablespoons corn oil
2 onions, thinly sliced
1 cinnamon stick
4 black peppercorns
2 black cardamom pods
1½ teaspoons garam masala
1½ teaspoons ginger pulp (page 17)
1½ teaspoons garlic pulp (page 17)
1 teaspoon ground coriander

2 teaspoons chilli powder
225 ml / 8 fl oz plain runny yoghurt
salt
2 tablespoons chopped fresh coriander leaves
2 fresh green chillies, chopped

for the garnish:
1 tablespoon finely shredded fresh ginger
1 red onion, diced
whole coriander sprigs
2-3 tablespoons olive oil (optional)

1 In a large bowl, soak the cracked wheat overnight in plenty of water to cover generously.

2 Cut the skinless chicken pieces into strips, about 1 cm / ½ inch thick.

3 Heat the corn oil in a kadahi, wok or deep frying pan and fry the onions with the whole spices over a low-to-moderate heat until the onions are golden brown.

4 Meanwhile, in a bowl, mix together the garam masala, ginger, garlic, ground coriander, chilli powder, yoghurt and salt to taste. Mix the chicken pieces into the yoghurt mixture.

5 When the onions are ready, pour the chicken mixture into the onions and stir-fry over a moderate heat for a minute or two.

6 Partly cover the pan with a lid and let the chicken cook for 7-10 minutes, stirring occasionally.

Remove the pan from the heat and set aside.

7 Drain the cracked wheat, place it in a food processor and grind for about 1-1 ½ minutes, gradually adding 2 cups of water to loosen the mixture.

8 Return the chicken to the heat and add the cracked wheat. Stir-fry over a low-to-moderate heat for 5-7 minutes. Keep stirring so that it does not stick to the bottom of the pan.

9 Add half the fresh coriander and half the green chillies. If you feel the consistency is too thick (it should be like a thick soup), add a little more water. Adjust the seasoning to taste.

10 Transfer to a warmed serving plate and sprinkle with the remaining chillies and the shredded ginger, diced red onion, coriander sprigs and, if you like, some olive oil.

Cracked Wheat with Strips of Chicken served with Naan (page 124)

CHAR-GRILLED LEMON CHICKEN

SERVES 4

PREPARATION
about 20 minutes
COOKING
10-15 minutes

Calories per serving *258*
Total fat *High*
Saturated fat *Medium*
Protein *High*
Carbohydrate *Low*
Cholesterol per serving
126 mg
Vitamins *A, B group, C, E*
Minerals *Potassium, Iron,*
Zinc, Selenium

1 small chicken
1 tablespoon olive oil
1 ½ teaspoons garlic pulp (page 17)
grated zest of 1 and juice of 2 lemons
salt
1 teaspoon crushed dried red chillies

for the garnish:
bunch of watercress
1 lemon, sliced
8-10 cherry tomatoes
1 tablespoon chopped fresh coriander leaves

1   Preheat a moderate grill. Quarter the chicken and remove the skin. Using a sharp knife, make small slashes diagonally across the flesh to let flavours and heat penetrate.

2   In a small bowl, mix together the oil, garlic pulp, the lemon zest and juice and salt to taste. Brush this mixture all over the chicken pieces and then sprinkle it with the crushed dried red chillies.

3   Grill for 10-15 minutes, turning the pieces halfway through. Check with a sharp knife or a skewer to see that the chicken is completely cooked (the juices run clear).

4   Serve on a bed of watercress, garnished with the lemon slices, tomatoes and coriander.

GRILLED CHICKEN KEBABS

SERVES 4

PREPARATION
15-20 minutes,
plus 3 hours'
marinating
COOKING
15-20 minutes

Calories per serving *308*
Total fat *High*
Saturated fat *High*
Protein *High*
Carbohydrate *Low*
Cholesterol per serving
113 mg
Vitamins *B group*
Minerals *Potassium, Iron,*
Zinc, Iodine

450 g / 1 lb skinless boned chicken
175 ml / 6 fl oz low-fat plain runny yoghurt
2 tablespoons lemon juice
1½ teaspoons garlic pulp (page 17)
1½ teaspoons chilli powder
1½ teaspoons ginger pulp (page 17)

salt
2 tablespoons finely chopped fresh coriander leaves
1 tablespoon corn oil
plain boiled basmati rice, to serve
1 lime, sliced, for garnish

1   Cut the chicken into 3-5 cm / 1½-2 inch cubes and set aside.

2   In a large mixing bowl, whisk the yoghurt with the lemon juice, garlic, chilli, ginger, salt to taste and 300 ml / ½ pint water.

3   Drop the chicken pieces into the yoghurt mixture, followed by half the fresh coriander, and mix everything together. Leave to marinate at room temperature for at least 3 hours.

4   Preheat the grill to very hot. Pick out the chicken pieces, shaking off as much marinade as possible, and place on 4 skewers. Place the skewers on a heatproof dish and brush with the oil.

5   Turn the grill down to moderate. Place the skewers under the grill and cook for 7-10 minutes, then turn them over to ensure even cooking. Any burn marks that appear will only help by giving the chicken a char-grilled flavour.

6   Served on a bed of boiled rice, garnished with the remaining fresh coriander and a few lime slices.

BAKED COCONUT CHICKEN WITH SPICY MASHED PARSNIP

This spicy parsnip has an intriguing sweet-and-sour flavour and makes a delicious alternative to mashed potato as an accompaniment.

1 chicken, weighing about 1.5 kg / 3¼ lb
1½ tablespoons olive oil
1 onion, diced
1 bay leaf
2 cloves
2.5-cm / 1-inch piece of cinnamon stick
3 garlic cloves, crushed
1 teaspoon shredded ginger
100 ml / 3½ fl oz coconut milk
1 teaspoon chilli powder
1 teaspoon sugar
1 tablespoon lemon juice
salt

1 tablespoon chopped fresh coriander leaves
30 g / 1 oz cashew nuts
30 g / 1 oz sultanas

for the spicy mashed parsnip:
900 g / 2 lb parsnips, coarsely chopped
2 tablespoons olive oil
½ red pepper, deseeded and diced
1 green chilli, chopped
1 teaspoon mango powder
1 tablespoon chopped fresh coriander leaves
1 tablespoon chopped fresh mint

SERVES 4

PREPARATION
about 30 minutes
COOKING
40-45 minutes

Calories per serving 640
Total fat *Medium*
Saturated fat *Low*
Protein *High*
Carbohydrate *Low*
Cholesterol per serving
201 mg
Vitamins *B group, C, E*
Minerals *Calcium,*
Potassium, Iron, Zinc,
Selenium, Iodine

1   Preheat the oven to 190°C/375°F/gas 5. Skin the chicken and cut it into about 8 pieces.

2   Heat the oil in a kadahi, wok or deep frying pan over a moderate heat and add the onion, bay leaf, cloves, cinnamon, garlic, ginger, 3 tablespoons of the coconut milk, the chilli powder, sugar and lemon juice with 150 ml / ¼ pint of water and salt to taste. Cook until semi-dry.

3   Add the fresh coriander, cashew nuts and sultanas. Stir-fry for about 2 minutes over a low heat.

4   Now add the chicken pieces, followed by the remaining coconut milk. Transfer this to an oven-proof dish and cook in the oven for 35-40 minutes, until the chicken is cooked through.

5   While the chicken is cooking, make the spicy mashed parsnip: cook the parsnips in boiling salted for about 15-18 minutes, until tender. Drain well

and mash them using a potato masher. Place in a mixing bowl and add the olive oil, the diced red pepper, green chilli, mango powder, coriander, mint and salt to taste. Blend everything together and serve with the baked chicken.

CHICKEN BREASTS WITH MANGO SAUCE

Try to choose thin chicken breasts for this dish as they need to be grilled fairly quickly. It helps to remove the little 'fillets' on the underside of the breasts (use them for another purpose, such as a salad, since they cook in seconds), as this makes it easier to flatten the breasts out.

SERVES 4

PREPARATION
about 20 minutes
COOKING
about 15 minutes

Calories per serving *174*
Total fat *High*
Saturated fat *Medium*
Protein *High*
Carbohydrate *Low*
Cholesterol per serving *35 mg*
Vitamins *A, B group, C, E*
Minerals *Potassium*

2 boneless skinless chicken breasts
1 tablespoon olive oil
2 tablespoons lemon juice
1 teaspoon chopped fresh coriander leaves, to garnish
1 fresh green chilli, finely chopped, to garnish

for the mango sauce:
2 tablespoons sunflower oil
large pinch of onion seeds

6 curry leaves
3 tomatoes, sliced
1 teaspoon ginger pulp (page 17)
1 teaspoon garlic pulp (page 17)
2 tablespoons mango chutney
1 teaspoon chilli powder
salt
1 tablespoon chopped fresh coriander leaves
1 tablespoon low-fat crème fraîche

1 Rinse the chicken breasts and pat them dry. Remove the fillets and flatten the breasts out as described above. Using a sharp knife, make 2 diagonal slits on each breast to allow the flavours and heat to penetrate the flesh more easily.

2 In a small bowl, mix the olive oil, lemon juice and a little salt. Using a pastry brush, brush the mixture all over the breasts and chill.

3 Make the mango sauce: heat the sunflower oil in a kadahi, wok or deep frying pan over a moderate heat and fry the onion seeds and curry leaves for about 30 seconds. Then add the sliced tomato and fry for about 2 minutes. Add the ginger, garlic, mango chutney, chilli powder, salt to taste and fresh coriander. Stir-fry for about 3 minutes. Finally, add the crème fraîche and remove from the heat. Keep warm.

4 Preheat the grill to moderate and grill the chicken breasts for 3-4 minutes on either side, until light golden brown, basting occasionally.

5 Serve the chicken breasts on a warmed serving dish, with the sauce poured all around them and garnished with the coriander and green chillies. If you like, you can cut the breasts across at an angle into slices, then fan the slices out.

Chicken Breasts with Mango Sauce served with Chapati (page 124)

HOT AND SPICY CHICKEN STIR-FRY WITH SESAME

The good thing about a quick stir-fry is that you can use up any left-over roast chicken pieces and serve them incorporated in a completely new dish. Alternatively, you can, of course, start from scratch with fresh boned chicken pieces. If using cooked chicken, omit step 3 and just add it with the vegetables.

175 g / 6 oz boneless, skinless chicken
2 tablespoons corn oil
1 teaspoon garlic pulp (page 17)
1 teaspoon ginger pulp (page 17)
1 teaspoon chilli powder
1 teaspoon ground coriander
salt

1 leek, sliced
8-10 mushrooms, thickly sliced
½ green pepper, deseeded and coarsely chopped
½ red pepper, deseeded and coarsely chopped
2 tablespoons chopped fresh coriander leaves
1 tablespoon white sesame seeds
1 tablespoon lemon juice

SERVES 4

PREPARATION
about 15 minutes
COOKING
about 10 minutes

Calories per serving *113*
Total fat *High*
Saturated fat *Low*
Protein *High*
Carbohydrate *Low*
Cholesterol per serving
31 mg
Vitamins *A, B group, C, E*
Minerals *Potassium, Iron, Zinc*

1   Cut the chicken into bite-sized pieces.

2   In a bowl, combine the corn oil with the garlic, ginger, chilli powder, ground coriander and salt to taste. Pour this mixture into a kadahi, wok or deep frying pan and place over a moderate heat. Stir-fry the spices for about 30 seconds.

3   Add the prepared chicken pieces and toss to blend everything together. Continue stir-frying in this way over moderate heat for 5-7 minutes.

4   Add the sliced leek, the mushrooms and the chopped green and red peppers, together with half the chopped coriander, and stir-fry for about 5 minutes more.

5   Just before serving, add the sesame seeds and sprinkle with the lemon juice. Serve garnished with the remaining coriander.

Hot and Spicy Chicken Stir-Fry with Sesame served with Naan (page 124)

ROAST CHICKEN WITH LIME AND HERBS

SERVES 4

PREPARATION
*about 20 minutes,
plus 1 hour's
marinating*
COOKING
35-40 minutes

Calories per serving *186*
Total fat *Medium*
Saturated fat *Low*
Protein *High*
Carbohydrate *Low*
Cholesterol per serving
79 mg
Vitamins *B group, C, E*
Minerals *Potassium, Iron,
Zinc, Iodine*

*4 chicken quarters
2 tablespoons virgin olive oil
1 teaspoon ginger pulp (page 17)
1 teaspoon garlic pulp (page 17)
4 tablespoons lime juice
1 green chilli, chopped
6 tablespoons chopped fresh coriander leaves*

*1 tablespoon chopped fresh mint, plus more
shredded leaves for garnish
salt
1 teaspoon freshly ground black pepper
2 tomatoes, sliced
lime wedges. to serve*

1   Remove the skin from the chicken, prick it all over with a fork and set aside in a heatproof dish.
2   In a bowl, mix together the olive oil, ginger, garlic, lime juice, green chilli, fresh coriander, mint and salt to taste. Mix well and pour it over the chicken pieces. Use a brush to ensure they are evenly coated. Sprinkle with the ground black pepper and top with the sliced tomatoes. Cover with foil and leave to marinate for about 1 hour.
3   Preheat the oven to 190°C/375°F/gas 5. Cook for 35-40 minutes, basting once or twice. Serve with lime wedges, garnished with shredded mint.

HOT ACHAARI CHICKEN

Achaar *means pickle and this chicken dish uses spices which are more usually used to make pickles.*

SERVES 4

PREPARATION
about 20 minutes
COOKING
about 15 minutes

Calories per serving *142*
Total fat *High*
Saturated fat *Low*
Protein *High*
Carbohydrate *Low*
Cholesterol per serving
39 mg
Vitamins *B group*
Minerals *Iron, Selenium,
Potassium*

*225 g / 8 oz skinless chicken breast fillet
2 tablespoons olive oil
1 heaped teaspoon mixed equal parts cumin seeds,
crushed coriander seeds, mustard seeds, onion
seeds, fennel seeds and fenugreek seeds
6-8 whole curry leaves
2 onions, finely chopped
1 teaspoon ginger pulp (page 17)
1 teaspoon garlic pulp (page 17)*

*1 teaspoon chilli powder
¼ teaspoon turmeric
1 teaspoon ground cumin
1 teaspoon ground coriander
1 tablespoon tomato purée
salt
2 fresh red chillies, chopped
1 tablespoon chopped fresh coriander leaves*

1   Cut the chicken into cubes and set aside.
2   Heat the oil in a kadahi, wok or deep frying pan and fry seeds over moderate heat for 40 seconds.
3   Add the curry leaves, onions, ginger, garlic, chilli powder, turmeric, ground cumin, ground coriander and tomato purée, with 150 ml / ¼ pint of water and salt to taste, followed by the chicken. Stir-fry for about 3 minutes.
4   Lower the heat, cover the pan and cook over a very low heat for 5-7 minutes, stirring occasionally.
5   Just before serving, stir in the chopped chillies and the fresh coriander.

Roast Chicken with Lime and Herbs

GINGER AND LEMON CHICKEN

This dish not only tastes wonderful but also looks very colourful when garnished with fresh coriander, cherry tomatoes and, of course, shredded ginger.

SERVES 4

PREPARATION
about 20 minutes
COOKING
15-20 minutes

Calories per serving *127*
Total fat *Medium*
Saturated fat *Medium*
Protein *High*
Carbohydrate *Low*
Cholesterol per serving
48 mg
Vitamins *A, B group, C, E*
Minerals *Calcium,*
Potassium, Iron, Zinc,
Iodine

225 g / 8 oz skinless boned chicken pieces
125 ml / 4 fl oz plain low-fat runny yoghurt
2 tablespoons lemon juice
1½ teaspoons ginger pulp
1 teaspoon dried crushed red chillies
1½ teaspoons ground coriander
½ teaspoon turmeric
salt
125 g / 4½ oz virtually fat-free fromage frais
1 tablespoon corn oil

1 bay leaf
8-10 red and green peppercorns
2-3 green cardamom pods
1 tablespoon chopped fresh coriander

for the garnish:
few sprigs of fresh coriander
8 cherry tomatoes, halved
1 tablespoon shredded ginger

1 Cut the chicken into cubes and set aside. In a medium-sized mixing bowl, blend together the yoghurt, lemon juice, ginger, dried crushed red chillies, ground coriander, turmeric, salt to taste and the fromage frais. Mix everything together well and set aside

2 In a frying pan, heat the oil with the bay leaf, peppercorns and cardamoms over a moderate heat for about 2 minutes until aromatic. Pour in the yoghurt mixture and cook for about 1 minute.

3 Add the cubes of chicken, lower the heat and cook for 7-10 minutes, stirring and checking occasionally to ensure it hasn't caught on the bottom of the pan.

4 Add the fresh coriander and stir for about 2 minutes, then transfer to a warmed serving dish.

5 Garnish with the coriander sprigs, the tomatoes and shredded ginger, and serve hot.

Ginger and Lemon Chicken served with Rice with Desiccated Coconut (page 128)

ROAST CHICKEN QUARTERS WITH A SPICY HONEY SAUCE

This chicken has a sauce that is sweet yet tangy, as it contains some tamarind. It can be served with Rice with Pine Nuts (page 128) and a vegetable stir-fry.

SERVES 4

PREPARATION
about 15 minutes
COOKING
about 45 minutes

Calories per serving *280*
Total fat *Medium*
Saturated fat *Low*
Protein *High*
Carbohydrate *Low*
Cholesterol per serving
113 mg
Vitamins *B group, C, E*
Minerals *Potassium, Iron,*
Zinc, Selenium

1 small chicken
1 tablespoon tamarind pulp (see page 15)
2 tablespoons tomato purée
2 tablespoons honey
1 teaspoon ginger pulp (page 17)
1 teaspoon chilli powder
1½ teaspoons ground coriander
salt

2 teaspoons sugar
2 tablespoons chopped fresh coriander leaves
2 fresh red chillies, diced
150 g / 5 oz canned chickpeas, drained
2 tablespoons corn oil
4-6 curry leaves
large pinch of onion seeds

1   Preheat the oven to 190°C/375°F/gas 5. Remove the skin from the chicken and quarter the bird.

2   In a bowl, mix the tamarind sauce, tomato purée, honey, ginger, chilli powder, ground coriander, salt to taste, sugar, half of the fresh coriander and half of the red chillies, the drained chickpeas and 300 ml / ½ pint of water to form a thick paste.

3   Heat the oil in a saucepan over a moderate heat and fry the curry leaves with the onion seeds for about 45 seconds. Then pour in the honey sauce and cook for about 2 minutes. Remove the pan from the heat.

4   Using a pastry brush, brush half of the sauce over the chicken pieces. Place the chicken in the oven for 35-40 minutes, basting occasionally.

5   Serve with the remainder of the sauce poured over the top and garnished with the remaining fresh coriander and dried chillies.

FRIED CHICKEN WITH FRESH CORIANDER AND LEMON

SERVES 4

PREPARATION
about 15 minutes
COOKING
about 15 minutes

225 g / 8 oz skinless boned chicken
2 tablespoons corn oil
2 onions, sliced
½ teaspoon cumin seeds
8 curry leaves

3 garlic cloves
1½ teaspoons shredded ginger
1 teaspoon crushed dried red chillies
salt
1 tablespoon lemon juice

10-12 mange-tout peas
60 g / 2 oz frozen sweetcorn kernels
2 fresh red chillies, deseeded and sliced lengthwise

1   Prepare the chicken by cutting it into strips.
2   In a kadahi, wok or deep frying pan, heat the oil over a moderate heat and fry the onion with the cumin seeds and curry leaves for about 2 minutes.
3   Add the garlic, ginger, dried chillies, salt to taste and lemon juice. Then add the chicken and turn

1 tablespoon finely chopped fresh coriander leaves, plus more whole leaves to garnish

the heat down slightly. Stir-fry for 5-7 minutes, until all the chicken pieces are cooked through.
4   Add the mange-tout, sweetcorn, fresh chillies and the fresh coriander. Stir-fry for 2 or 3 minutes more before serving, garnished with some whole coriander leaves.

Calories per serving 160
Total fat *Medium*
Saturated fat *Low*
Protein *High*
Carbohydrate *Low*
Cholesterol per serving
39 mg
Vitamins A, *B group, C, E*
Minerals *Potassium, Iron*

CHICKEN BREASTS WITH FRUITY SAFFRON SAUCE

Saffron – reputedly the most expensive spice in the world – has a beautiful aroma. In India and Pakistan it is used for special dishes, such as biryanis *and some elaborate desserts. Here a delicious saffron sauce is poured over chicken breasts with nuts and fruit.*

4 chicken breast fillets, skinned
1 tablespoon tomato purée
3 tablespoons plain low-fat runny yoghurt
1 teaspoon garlic pulp
½ teaspoon garam masala
¼ teaspoon ground fennel seeds
¼ teaspoon ground cardamom seeds
4 tablespoons virtually fat-free fromage frais
1 teaspoon ground almonds

½ teaspoon chilli powder
1 tablespoon lemon juice
salt
¼ teaspoon saffron strands
1 tablespoon corn oil
1 bay leaf
1 cinnamon stick
30 g / 1 oz sultanas
30 g / 1 oz flaked almonds

1   Using a sharp knife, make 2 slashes into each chicken breast without cutting right through. This will help the flavours and the heat to penetrate.
2   In a bowl, blend together the tomato purée, yoghurt, garlic, garam masala, fennel, cardamom, fromage frais, ground almonds, chilli powder, lemon juice, salt to taste, and the saffron with 4 tablespoons of water.
3   Heat the oil in a deep frying pan and fry the bay

leaf and cinnamon stick for about 30 seconds. Then add the sauce mixture together with 150 ml / ¼ pint water and bring to the boil. Pour this over the top of the chicken breasts and leave to marinate for about 1 hour.
4   Preheat the oven to 190°C/375°F/gas 5. Place the chicken with the sauce in a heatproof dish and sprinkle over the sultanas and almonds. Cook in the preheated oven for 15-20 minutes.

SERVES 4

PREPARATION
*about 15 minutes,
plus 1 hour's
marinating*
COOKING
20-25 minutes

Calories per serving *217*
Total fat *High*
Saturated fat *Low*
Protein *High*
Carbohydrate *Low*
Cholesterol per serving
56 mg
Vitamins *B group, C, E*
Minerals *Potassium, Iron, Selenium*

TANDOORI CHICKEN WITH RADISH SALAD

Tandoori chicken is probably one of the most popular of all dishes from the subcontinent. Ideally it should be cooked in a clay oven (the tandoor*). As this is not possible in ordinary households, however, I suggest you preheat your oven to the highest possible temperature.*

SERVES 4

PREPARATION
*about 15 minutes,
plus 3 hours'
marinating*
COOKING
15-18 minutes

Calories per serving *229*
Total fat *Low*
Saturated fat *Low*
Protein *High*
Carbohydrate *Low*
Cholesterol per serving
137 mg
Vitamins *A, B group, C, E*
Minerals *Calcium,
Potassium, Iron, Zinc,
Selenium, Iodine*

**1 chicken, weighing about
1.5 kg / 3 ¼ lb
150 ml / ¼ pint plain low-fat runny yoghurt
1 teaspoon ginger pulp (page 17)
1 teaspoon garlic pulp (page 17)
1 tablespoon tomato purée
1 teaspoon paprika
2 tablespoons lemon juice
1½ teaspoons ground coriander
1 teaspoon garam masala
salt**

**corn oil, for greasing the baking tray
lemon or lime wedges, to serve**

**for the radish salad:
4 large leaves from an iceberg lettuce, shredded
1 red onion, sliced
½ cucumber, peeled and sliced
2 tomatoes, quartered
4 whole green chillies
115 g / 4 oz radishes or mooli (page 20), sliced**

1 Skin the chicken and cut it into 8 pieces. Using a sharp knife, make 2 deep slashes in each piece without cutting right through, to allow flavours and heat to penetrate the flesh.

2 Pour the low-fat yoghurt into a large bowl. Add the ginger, garlic, tomato purée, paprika, lemon juice, ground coriander seeds, garam masala and 225 ml / 8 fl oz water with salt to taste. Mix well together and pour over the chicken pieces. Leave to marinate for at least 3 hours or overnight.

3 When ready to cook, preheat the oven to its highest possible temperature. Lift the chicken pieces from the marinade, place them on a greased

baking tray and place it in the hot oven. Cook the chicken for 15-18 minutes, checking once or twice to make sure it is not browning too fast. If burn marks begin to appear too rapidly, just turn the oven down slightly.

4 While the chicken is cooking, make the salad by mixing all the ingredients, then arrange it on 4 serving plates.

5 Check to see that the chicken is cooked right through by piercing with the point of a knife at the thickest part of the flesh (the juices should run clear rather than pink) and serve with the salad and wedges of lemon or lime.

Tandoori Chicken with Radish Salad

SPAGHETTI WITH MINI CHICKEN KOFTA

Spaghetti was always a great favourite of ours when we were children living in Pakistan. My mother would serve it with spicy minced lamb and a tomato chutney. This is my healthier version of that childhood staple.

225 g / 8 oz spaghetti

for the kofta:
275 g / 10 oz skinless boned chicken, cubed
1½ teaspoons ginger pulp (page 17)
1½ teaspoons garlic pulp (page 17)
1 teaspoon ground cumin
2 teaspoons ground coriander
1 teaspoon chilli powder
1 teaspoon mango powder
salt
2 tablespoons chopped fresh coriander leaves
1 fresh red chilli, diced
1 small egg, lightly beaten
2 tablespoons corn oil

for the spiced tomato sauce:
4 tablespoons tomato purée
2 tablespoons virtually fat-free fromage frais
1 teaspoon ground coriander
1 teaspoon garlic pulp (page 17)
1 teaspoon ginger pulp (page 17)
1 teaspoon chilli powder
1 teaspoon salt
1 tablespoon corn oil
4 curry leaves
¼ teaspoon onion seeds

for the garnish:
1 fresh red chilli, chopped
few fresh mint leaves, shredded
freshly ground black pepper

SERVES 4

PREPARATION
about 25 minutes
COOKING
about 30 minutes

Calories per serving *266*
Total fat *High*
Saturated fat *Low*
Protein *High*
Carbohydrate *Low*
Cholesterol per serving *122 mg*
Vitamins *A, B group, C, E*
Minerals *Calcium, Potassium, Iron, Zinc, Selenium, Iodine*

1 First prepare the kofta: mix together with the chicken, ginger, garlic, cumin, ground coriander, chilli powder, mango powder and salt to taste. Place in a saucepan and pour in 600 ml / 1 pint of water. Bring to the boil, lower the heat and cook for 12-15 minutes, or until the liquid has fully evaporated and the chicken pieces are cooked. Allow to cool.

2 When the chicken is cool, grind it in the food processor with the fresh coriander and the red chilli until the chicken is minced.

3 Bind the mince together by adding the beaten egg. Break off small pieces about the size of a golf ball and mould them into about 20-25 ball shapes.

4 Heat the oil in a small frying pan (preferably non-stick) and fry the koftas until golden brown. Remove from the heat and set aside.

5 Make the sauce: in a bowl, mix the tomato purée, fromage frais, coriander, garlic, ginger, chilli and salt to taste with 150 ml / ¼ pint of water. Heat the oil in a saucepan over a moderate heat with the curry leaves and onion seeds. Lower the heat and pour in the sauce. Bring to the boil and cook for a further 1 minute. Add the cooked koftas to the sauce and keep it warm.

6 Cook the spaghetti in a large pan of boiling salted water until just tender. Drain.

7 Pour the sauce over the spaghetti and serve it with the garnish.

Spaghetti with Mini Chicken Kofta

CHICKEN WITH FENUGREEK AND TOMATOES

Chicken goes extremely well with fenugreek and tomatoes. Fenugreek has a beautiful aroma and the tomato base gives this curry a rich flavour.

SERVES 4

PREPARATION
about 25 minutes
COOKING
about 20 minutes

Calories per serving *194*
Total fat *High*
Saturated fat *Low*
Protein *High*
Carbohydrate *Low*
Cholesterol per serving
51 mg
Vitamins *A, B group, C, E*
Minerals *Potassium, Iron, Zinc*

225 g / 8 oz skinless boned chicken
3 tablespoons fresh fenugreek
1 tablespoon sesame seeds
1 level tablespoon tamarind pulp (page 15)
1 teaspoon chilli powder
salt
1 teaspoon ground coriander
½ teaspoon ground cumin
1 teaspoon ginger pulp (page 17)

1 teaspoon garlic pulp (page 17)
2 teaspoons sugar
2 tablespoons corn oil
¼ teaspoon mixed onion seeds and fenugreek seeds
4-6 curry leaves
6 tomatoes, coarsely chopped
2 tablespoons chopped fresh coriander leaves
1 fresh green chilli, chopped

1 Cut the chicken into cubes and set aside. Break the leaves off the fresh fenugreek, wash them and pat dry.

2 Place the sesame seeds in a spice grinder and grind to a fine powder. Place in a small bowl and add the tamarind, chilli, salt to taste, the ground coriander, cumin, ginger, garlic and sugar. Using a spoon, mix with about 2 tablespoons of water to make a paste.

3 In a kadahi, wok or deep frying pan, heat the oil and stir-fry the mixed onion and fenugreek seeds together with the curry leaves over a moderate heat for about 1 minute. Add to this the tomatoes, followed by the spice paste. Stir to mix everything together and throw in the chicken pieces. Stir-fry for 2 minutes.

4 Add the fenugreek leaves, lower the heat, cover and cook for 10 minutes, stirring occasionally.

5 Remove the lid and stir in the chilli and one tablespoon of the fresh coriander. Cook for 2 minutes more and serve hot, garnished with the remaining fresh coriander.

Chicken with Fenugreek and Tomatoes

CHICKEN KADAHI

Traditionally kadahi *(see page 9) were made of cast iron, but nowadays they are more often stainless steel. These are very attractive to serve from at the dining table.*

SERVES 4

PREPARATION
about 15 minutes
COOKING
20-25 minutes

Calories per serving *153*
Total fat *High*
Saturated fat *Low*
Protein *High*
Carbohydrate *Low*
Cholesterol per serving
51 mg
Vitamins *B group, C, E*
Minerals *Potassium, Iron,
Zinc*

225 g / 8 oz skinless boned chicken
2 tablespoons corn oil
2 onions, diced
1 teaspoon garlic pulp (page 17)
1 teaspoon ginger pulp (page 17)
1 teaspoon ground coriander
1 teaspoon chilli powder

salt
2 tablespoons chopped fresh coriander leaves
1 green pepper, deseeded and sliced
8 cherry tomatoes
½ teaspoon garam masala
1 teaspoon shredded ginger, to garnish
1 lime, cut into wedges

1 Cut the chicken into bite-sized cubes and set them aside.

2 Heat the oil in a kadahi, wok or deep frying pan over a moderate heat and fry the diced onions for about 3 minutes.

3 Add the chicken pieces and stir-fry to seal them.

4 Next add the ginger, garlic, ground coriander, chilli powder and salt to taste. Continue to stir-fry for a further 2 minutes. Add half the chopped fresh

coriander and about 300 ml / ½ pint of water. Reduce the heat and cook for 7-10 minutes, or until the sauce begins to thicken and the chicken is cooked. Add the green pepper, cherry tomatoes and garam masala, and stir-fry for a further 2 minutes.

5 Serve garnished with the shredded ginger and remaining fresh coriander. Squeeze the juice from a wedge of the lime over the chicken and serve with the remaining lime wedges.

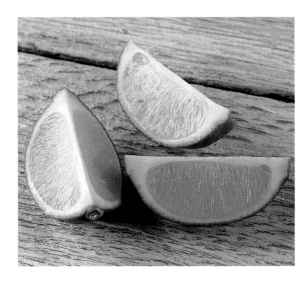

LAMB KEBABS
WITH A SPICY GINGER FILLING

These fruity delicious kebabs can be made with minced beef if you prefer. As an alternative to frying, you may grill them under a preheated moderate grill, after first brushing them lightly with oil.

450 g / 1 lb lean minced lamb
1 teaspoon ground cumin
1 teaspoon ground coriander
1 teaspoon garam masala
1 teaspoon ginger pulp (page 17)
1 teaspoon garlic pulp (page 17)
¼ teaspoon ground cardamom seeds
1 teaspoon chilli powder
1 tablespoon chopped fresh coriander
2 tablespoons chopped fresh mint
1 small onion, diced

salt
corn oil for brushing

for the filling:
1 tablespoon shredded ginger
1 green chilli, deseeded and chopped
1 red chilli, deseeded and chopped
2 tablespoons chopped fresh coriander leaves
2 tablespoons plain low-fat runny yoghurt
2 medium tomatoes, deseeded and diced

SERVES 4
(MAKES 10-12)

PREPARATION
about 30 minutes
COOKING
about 20 minutes

Calories per serving *200*
Total fat *High*
Saturated fat *High*
Protein *High*
Carbohydrate *Low*
Cholesterol per serving
84 mg
Vitamins *A, B group, C, E*
Minerals *Potassium, Iron,
Zinc, Iodine*

1   Start by placing the minced lamb, ground cumin, ground coriander, garam masala, ginger, garlic, cardamom, chilli powder, fresh coriander, mint and onion in a saucepan with salt to taste.

2   Using a fork, mix everything together thoroughly. Pour in 5 tablespoons of water, bring to a simmer and cook over a low heat, stirring occasionally, for 10-12 minutes until quite dry. Once the liquid has evaporated from the lamb, stir the mince until completely dry and remove from the heat. Leave to cool.

3   Make the filling by mixing together all the ingredients and set aside.

4   Place the cooled kebab mixture in the food processor and grind for 1-1½ minutes, until it is quite paste-like. Transfer it from the processor to a bowl and use your hand to mix it well together. Break off small balls and shape them into a round flat shape in the palm of your hand. Make a dimple in the middle with your thumb, fill this with about 1 teaspoon of the filling and fold the sides over to enclose the filling and make a flat round shape again. Repeat until you have made 10-12 kebabs. Place these on a tray.

5   Brush a non-stick frying pan with a little oil and fry the kebabs gently in batches, pressing them down well with a spatula, for about 40 seconds on each side.

HARA MASALA LAMB KEBABS

Hara masala means 'green spices' – here, spring onion, coriander leaves, mint and green chillies. These kebabs are excellent for picnics, as you can serve them sandwiched in buns like burgers. (See page 65.)

SERVES 4

PREPARATION
about 30 minutes
COOKING
15-20 minutes

Calories per serving *269*
Total fat *High*
Saturated fat *High*
Protein *High*
Carbohydrate *Low*
Cholesterol per serving
141 mg
Vitamins *B group, C, E*
Minerals *Potassium, Iron, Zinc, Iodine*

450 g / 1 lb lean minced lamb
4 spring onions, chopped
2 tablespoons chopped fresh coriander leaves
1 tablespoon chopped fresh mint, plus more sprigs to garnish
2-3 green chillies, chopped

1 teaspoon shredded ginger
1 teaspoon garlic pulp (page 17)
salt
1 small egg, lightly beaten
2-3 tablespoons corn oil
few leaves of endive, to garnish

1   Place the minced lamb in a food processor and grind it for about 30 seconds to get a finer texture. Add the spring onions, fresh coriander, mint, green chillies, ginger, garlic and salt to taste. Grind for about 1 minute more.

2   Remove the mixture from the processor and place it in a bowl. Blend in the egg and mix really well, either using your fingers or a fork.

3   Break off small balls of the mixture and make them into 12-16 flat round shapes in your palm.

4   Heat half of the oil in a non-stick frying pan over a moderate heat and fry half the kebabs slowly, turning twice and pressing them down as they cook, until well browned. As the kebabs are cooked, remove them from the pan and drain them on paper towels to absorb any excess oil. Cook the remaining kebabs in the same way.

5   Serve garnished with endive and mint sprigs.

LAMB PULAO

SERVES 4

PREPARATION
*about 30 minutes,
plus 1 hour's
marinating*
COOKING
*about 45 minutes,
plus 5 minutes'
resting*

Calories per serving *592*
Total fat *High*
Saturated fat *Medium*
Protein *High*

450 g / 1 lb lean boned leg of lamb, cut into slices about 5 mm / ¼ in thick and 5 cm / 2 in long
225 ml / 8 fl oz plain low-fat runny yoghurt
2 tablespoons ground almonds
¼ teaspoon ground cardamom seeds
1 teaspoon chilli powder
1 teaspoon garam masala
1 teaspoon ginger pulp (page 17)
1 teaspoon garlic pulp (page 17)
1 tablespoon desiccated coconut
3 tablespoons chopped fresh coriander leaves

3-4 tablespoons corn oil
2 onions, sliced
60 g / 2 oz green beans, cut into short lengths
2 fresh tomatoes, chopped
1 bay leaf
2 cups of rice, washed
1 green chilli, chopped
1 red chilli, chopped
3 tablespoons lemon juice
½ teaspoon saffron strands

Previous pages: Spring Lamb Chops with Grilled Vegetables, Lamb Pulao served with Naan (page 124)

1   Place the lamb slices in a large bowl and add the yoghurt, ground almonds, ground cardamom, chilli powder, garam masala, ginger, garlic, desiccated coconut and 1 tablespoon of the fresh coriander. Blend everything together and set aside to marinate for about 1 hour.

2   Heat the oil in a large saucepan over a moderate heat and fry the onions until golden. Then add the beans, tomatoes, bay leaf and the lamb mixture. Bring to a simmer, lower the heat and cook, covered, for 7-10 minutes, stirring occasionally.

3   Pour in the rice and, using a slotted spoon, gently stir it around. Add the remaining fresh coriander, the green and red chillies, the lemon juice and the saffron strands. Pour in 3 cups of water and bring it to the boil. Lower the heat, cover with a lid and cook for 10-15 minutes, or until the water is fully absorbed and the rice is cooked.

4   Leave the dish to stand off the heat for about 5 minutes before serving.

Carbohydrate *Low*
Cholesterol per serving *85 mg*
Vitamins *A, B group, C, E*
Minerals *Potassium, Iron, Zinc, Iodine*

SPRING LAMB CHOPS WITH GRILLED VEGETABLES

I use a grill pan just to brown the chops and then finish them in the oven for about 20 minutes.

8 spring lamb chops, each 85-125 g / 3-4½ oz
2 teaspoons garlic pulp (page 17)
2 teaspoons ginger pulp (page 17)
2 green chillies, finely chopped
4 tablespoons chopped fresh coriander leaves
salt
3 tablespoons lemon juice
1 tablespoon cornflour
corn oil, for brushing the pan

1 lime, quartered, to serve

for the grilled vegetables:
1 tablespoon olive oil
1 red onion, thickly sliced
1 green pepper, deseeded and quartered
2 firm plum tomatoes, halved
1 courgette, sliced thickly at an angle
½ teaspoon crushed dried chillies

SERVES 4

PREPARATION
about 25 minutes, plus 1 hour's marinating
COOKING
about 20 minutes

1   Trim the chops well by removing all the fat.

2   In a bowl, mix together the garlic, ginger, chillies, 3 tablespoons of the coriander, the salt, lemon juice, cornflour and 2 tablespoons of water. Place the chops on a plate and rub them all over with this mixture. Leave to marinate for about 1 hour.

3   Preheat the oven to 190°C/375°F/gas 5 and a ridged grill pan over moderate heat. Brush the pan lightly with oil. Place the chops in it and cook for about 1 minute on each side. Transfer to an oven-proof dish and cook the remaining chops in the same way. Put in the dish and cook in the oven for 15-20 minutes until the chops are cooked to taste.

4   About 10 minutes before the lamb is going to be ready, preheat the grill pan again for the vegetables. Brush lightly again with oil and start cooking the vegetables, pressing them down to get the char-grilled effect. Sprinkle with salt to taste and the crushed dried red chillies.

5   Remove the chops from the oven and serve with the vegetables alongside, garnished with the reserved fresh coriander and the lime quarters.

Calories per serving *238*
Total fat *High*
Saturated fat *High*
Protein *High*
Carbohydrate *Low*
Cholesterol per serving *74 mg*
Vitamins *A, B group, C, E*
Minerals *Potassium, Iron, Zinc*

STIR-FRIED STRIPS OF LAMB WITH PEPPERS AND PINEAPPLE

I feel lamb cut into strips is much quicker and easier to cook than the cubes traditional in Indian cuisine, especially in a dish like this in which the meat is stir-fried. You can use fresh pineapple, or good-quality canned pineapple in juice (not syrup) which also works well.

SERVES 4

PREPARATION
*about 20 minutes,
plus 30 minutes'
marinating*
COOKING
about 20 minutes

Calories per serving *203*
Total fat *High*
Saturated fat *Medium*
Protein *High*
Carbohydrate *Low*
Cholesterol per serving
42 mg
Vitamins *A, B group, C, E*
Minerals *Potassium, Iron,
Zinc*

225 g / 8 oz boned lamb
1 teaspoon ground coriander
1 teaspoon ground cumin
1 teaspoon mango powder
125 ml / 4 fl oz pineapple juice
1 teaspoon hot chilli sauce
1 teaspoon garlic pulp (page 17)
1 teaspoon ginger pulp (page 17)
¼ teaspoon turmeric

salt
2 tablespoons corn oil
½ red pepper, deseeded and cubed
½ green pepper, deseeded and cubed
12 chunks of pineapple
**1 tablespoon chopped fresh coriander leaves , plus
more sprigs for garnish**
1 tablespoon sesame seeds

1 Trim the lamb of any excess fat and cut it into strips about 5 mm / ¼ in thick and 5 cm / 2 in long. Place in a mixing bowl.

2 Add to the lamb the ground coriander, cumin, mango powder, pineapple juice, chilli sauce, garlic, ginger, turmeric and salt to taste. Blend everything well together and set aside for about 30 minutes.

3 Heat the oil in a kadahi, wok or deep frying pan over a moderate heat and drop the lamb into it.

Stir-fry for 2-3 minutes. Add about 150 ml / ¼ pint of water and bring to a simmer. Lower the heat, cover the pan and cook gently for 7-10 minutes, stirring occasionally.

4 Add the cubed peppers followed by the chunks of pineapple and the fresh coriander. Continue to stir-fry for a further 2 minutes.

5 Finally, garnish with the sesame seeds and coriander sprigs to serve.

Stir-Fried Strips of Lamb with Peppers and Pineapple

Vegetarian Dishes

MASOOR DHAL KHICHERI WITH VEGETABLES

Khicheri, *meaning rice cooked with lentils or other pulses, is the ancient word from which the British derived kedgeree. I have added vegetables to this version, which makes it a lot more interesting and tasty.*

SERVES 4-6

PREPARATION
about 20 minutes
COOKING
*25-30 minutes,
plus 5 minutes'
standing*

Calories per serving *407*
Total fat *Low*
Saturated fat *Low*
Protein *Medium*
Carbohydrate *High*
Cholesterol per serving
None
Vitamins *A, B₁, B₃, B₆, C,
E, Folate*
Minerals *Potassium, Iron,
Zinc*

2 cups of basmati rice
*1 cup of masoor dhal (salmon-coloured lentils,
page 23)*
2 tablespoons corn oil
4-6 curry leaves
¼ teaspoon mixed mustard seeds and onion seeds
1 small onion, sliced
1 teaspoon ginger pulp (page 17)

1 teaspoon garlic pulp (page 17)
½ teaspoon turmeric
1 medium carrot, diced
60 g / 2 oz shelled peas
60 g / 2 oz green beans, sliced into short lengths
salt
*1 tablespoon chopped fresh coriander leaves, plus
a few more sprigs for garnish*

1   Rinse the rice and masoor dhal well and leave them in a bowl of water to soak.

2   Heat the oil in a medium-sized heavy-based saucepan and fry the curry leaves and mustard and onion seeds with the onion for about 2 minutes.

3   Lower the heat and add the ginger, garlic, turmeric, carrot, peas, green beans and salt to taste.

Drain the rice and lentils and add these to the onion mixture. Stir for 2 minutes, then add 4 cups of water. Stir gently, adding the fresh coriander. When it begins to boil, lower the heat, cover and cook for 15-20 minutes.

4   Let stand off the heat, covered, for 5 minutes before serving, garnished with coriander sprigs.

COURGETTES AND AUBERGINES IN
A MINTY YOGHURT SAUCE

SERVES 4

PREPARATION
about 25 minutes
COOKING
25-30 minutes

1 medium aubergine
275 g / 10 oz plain low-fat runny yoghurt
1 teaspoon mint sauce
1 tablespoon chopped fresh mint
salt
1 teaspoon sugar
2 red chillies, chopped

1 tablespoon corn oil
6 whole curry leaves
¼ teaspoon white cumin seeds
1 large courgette, sliced
*1 tablespoon chopped fresh coriander leaves, to
garnish*

Previous pages: Okra with Baby Potatoes, Masoor Dhal Khicheri with Vegetables

1   Preheat the oven to 190°C/375°F/gas 5. Cut the top off the aubergine's stalk end and bake the aubergine in the oven for 20-25 minutes. When it is cool enough to handle, remove the skin and mash the flesh down with a fork.

2   In a large bowl, whisk the yoghurt and mix it with the aubergine flesh, mint sauce, fresh mint, sugar, red chillies and salt to taste. Set aside.

3   Heat the oil in a kadahi, wok or deep frying pan and fry the curry leaves, cumin seeds and courgette slices for about 1-1½ minutes over a moderate heat.

4   Pour the courgettes and their seasoned oil over the top of the yoghurt and aubergine mixture. Garnish with the fresh coriander to serve.

Calories per serving *85*
Total fat *Medium*
Saturated fat *Low*
Protein *High*
Carbohydrate *Low*
Cholesterol per serving *3 mg*
Vitamins *A, B₂, B₃, B₆, B₁₂, Folate, C*
Minerals *Calcium, Iron, Iodine*

OKRA WITH BABY POTATOES

450 g / 1 lb okra
10 baby potatoes
salt
2 tablespoons corn oil
3 onions, sliced
large pinch of onion seeds
large pinch of fennel seeds
large pinch of mustard seeds

½ teaspoon crushed dried red chillies
4 garlic cloves, sliced
2 tomatoes, quartered
2 tablespoons finely chopped fresh coriander leaves, plus a few more leaves for garnish
1 fresh green chilli, chopped
1 teaspoon lemon juice

Serves 4

Preparation
about 15 minutes
Cooking
25-30 minutes

Calories per serving *220*
Total fat *Medium*
Saturated fat *Low*
Protein *Low*
Carbohydrate *Medium*
Cholesterol per serving *None*
Vitamins *A, B₁, B₃, B₆, Folate, C, E*
Minerals *Calcium, Potassium, Iron, Zinc*

1   Cut the okra and potatoes in half. Cook the potatoes in boiling salted water until just soft but not mushy. Drain and set aside.

2   In a heavy-based saucepan over a moderate heat, heat the oil and fry the onions with the mixed seeds for 3-4 minutes, or until the onions are golden brown.

3   Add the crushed chillies, followed by the garlic, and stir-fry for a minute. Then add the tomatoes, okra, coriander, fresh green chilli, lemon juice and salt to taste. Lower the heat slightly, cover the pan and cook for 5-7 minutes.

4   Add the potatoes, cover and cook for a further 3-5 minutes. Serve garnished with more coriander.

LENTILS WITH VEGETABLES AND TAMARIND

Eaten widely in southern India, this lentil dish is traditionally served with rice or poori *(deep-fried bread). It can also be served in small bowls, as people drink it like a soup with their meal.*

SERVES 4

PREPARATION
about 20 minutes
COOKING
40-45 minutes

Calories per serving *150*
Total fat *Medium*
Saturated fat *Low*
Protein *Low*
Carbohydrate *High*
Cholesterol per serving
None
Vitamins *A, B₁, B₃, B₆,*
Folate, C, E
Minerals *Potassium, Iron*

2 tablespoons toor dhal (page 23)
2 tablespoons masoor dhal (page 23)
1 teaspoon ginger pulp (page 17)
1 teaspoon garlic pulp (page 17)
½ teaspoon turmeric
1 teaspoon chilli powder
1 heaped teaspoon ground coriander
salt
1 onion, chopped
3 curry leaves
30 g / 1 oz green beans, cut into pieces

1 carrot, diced
1 potato, diced
1 tablespoon tamarind pulp (page 15)
1 tablespoon brown sugar
2 tablespoons chopped fresh coriander leaves

for the tarka (seasoned oil):
1-2 tablespoons corn oil
½ teaspoon mustard seeds
3 whole dried red chillies
4-6 curry leaves

1 Mix together the toor and masoor dhal and wash them twice, running your fingers through them.

2 Drain them and put in a heavy-based saucepan. Add to this the ginger, garlic, turmeric, chilli powder, ground coriander, salt to taste, onion and curry leaves, followed by 600 ml / 1 pint of water. Bring to the boil, lower the heat and cook, partly covered, for 10-15 minutes, stirring occasionally. Check to see if the lentils have absorbed all the water; if they have, add more – up to 300 ml / ½ pint – and cook until the lentils are mushy enough to be mashed down to a paste, about 20-25 minutes.

3 Next add the green beans, carrots and potatoes, followed by a further 300 ml / ½ pint of water. Cook over a low heat for a further 5-7 minutes.

4 When the vegetables are cooked, add the tamarind, sugar and half the fresh coriander, followed by another 300 ml / ½ pint of water. Stir and bring to the boil. Remove from the heat and transfer to a warmed serving dish.

5 Make the tarka: heat the oil in a frying pan and fry the mustard seeds, dried red chillies and curry leaves. When the oil is hot and smoky, pour the tarka over the lentils.

6 Serve garnished with the remaining fresh coriander.

Lentils with Vegetables and Tamarind

VEGETABLE AND RED KIDNEY BEAN PULAO

This pulao *makes an excellent complete vegetarian meal in itself.*

2 cups of basmati rice

150 g / 5 oz canned red kidney beans

2 tablespoons corn oil

1 cinnamon stick

1 bay leaf

2 cloves

3 green cardamom pods

4 black peppercorns

1 onion, sliced

1 teaspoon ginger pulp (page 17)

1 teaspoon chilli powder

½ teaspoon turmeric

1 teaspoon garlic pulp (page 17)

1 teaspoon garam masala

1 teaspoon ground coriander seeds

60 g / 2 oz shelled peas

60 g / 2 oz cauliflower florets

1 carrot, sliced

1 courgette, sliced

2 tablespoons plain low-fat runny yoghurt

salt

2 tablespoons chopped coriander leaves

2 red chillies, sliced

1 tablespoon lemon juice

SERVES 4

PREPARATION
about 25 minutes
COOKING
*about 25 minutes,
plus 5 minutes'
resting*

Calories per serving *331*

Total fat *Low*

Saturated fat *Low*

Protein *Low*

Carbohydrate *High*

Cholesterol per serving
None

Vitamins *A, B$_1$, B$_3$, B$_6$,
Folate, C, E*

Minerals *Potassium, Iron*

1   Rinse the rice until the water runs clear. Leave it to soak while you prepare the other ingredients. Drain the liquid from the kidney beans and set them aside.

2   In a large heavy-based saucepan, heat the corn oil over a moderate heat. Add the whole cinnamon, bay leaves, cloves, cardamoms and peppercorns and cook for about 1 minute. Add the onions and fry these for about 2 minutes.

3   Lower the heat and add the ginger pulp, chilli powder, turmeric, garlic pulp, garam masala and ground coriander, followed by all the vegetables. Stir-fry for about 2 minutes, stirring in the yoghurt

towards the end of that time.

4   Drain the rice and add it with the beans to the pan. Using a slotted spoon, gently stir around in order to mix well without breaking up the rice. Add salt to taste, 1 tablespoon of the fresh coriander, the red chillies, lemon juice and 3 cups of water. Bring to the boil and turn the heat down to moderate. Cover the pan with a lid and cook until the water has been absorbed and the rice is cooked, about 10 - 15 minutes.

5   Let the pulao settle for about 5 minutes off the heat before serving, garnished with the remaining coriander leaves.

Vegetable and Red Kidney Bean Pulao

AUBERGINE WITH TOMATO AND ONION

Aubergines are very popular in Indian cooking and are used in a variety of ways. This particular recipe goes very well with freshly made chapati *(see page 124) and Mango and Apple Chutney (see page 139).*

SERVES 4

PREPARATION
about 20 minutes
COOKING
about 15 minutes

Calories per serving *105*
Total fat *High*
Saturated fat *Low*
Protein *Low*
Carbohydrate *Low*
Cholesterol per serving
None
Vitamins *B₃, B₆, Folate, C, E*
Minerals *Potassium, Iron*

1 large aubergine
2 onions
2 tablespoons corn oil
large pinch of mustard seeds
4 curry leaves
1 tablespoon tomato purée
1 tablespoon ground coriander

1 teaspoon garlic pulp (page 17)
1 teaspoon ginger pulp (page 17)
1 tablespoon lemon juice
salt
1 tablespoon chopped fresh coriander leaves
2 firm tomatoes, deseeded and diced
1 green chilli, chopped

1 Wash the aubergine, cut it into very small pieces and place these in a bowl. Chop the onions very finely.

2 Heat the oil in a medium-sized saucepan over a moderate heat and add the mustard seeds, curry leaves and the onion. Lower the heat and add the tomato purée, followed by the ground coriander, garlic, ginger, lemon juice and salt to taste, stirring continuously. Cook, stirring, for 3-5 minutes.

3 Next add the aubergine and continue to stir-fry for a further 2 minutes. Stir in 150 ml / ¼ pint of water, cover and cook over a low heat for 5-7 minutes, stirring occasionally.

4 Next add the fresh coriander and the tomatoes, followed by the green chilli. Stir gently for a minute or so, and serve.

Aubergine with Tomato and Onion served with Mango and Apple Chutney (page 139) and Chapati (page 124)

GRILLED VEGETABLES IN A PANCAKE ROLL

Grilled vegetables have become very popular in the last few years. I find that wrapping them in a spicy pancake roll is a delicious way of serving them, either as snacks or in large quantities with a salad for a main meal.

SERVES 4

PREPARATION
*25-30 minutes,
plus 30 minutes'
standing*
COOKING
about 30 minutes

Calories per serving *382*
Total fat *Medium*
Saturated fat *Low*
Protein *High*
Carbohydrate
Cholesterol per serving
183 mg
Vitamins *A, B group, C, E*
Minerals *Potassium, Iron*

1 red onion, sliced
1 large green pepper, deseeded and sliced
1 large orange pepper, deseeded and sliced
1 courgette, sliced
2 tomatoes, sliced
1 tablespoon olive oil
1 teaspoon fresh fenugreek
4 curry leaves
1 teaspoon crushed dried red chillies
salt

for the raita:
225 ml / 8 fl oz plain low-fat runny yoghurt
2 tablespoons clear honey

2 fresh red chillies, chopped
2 tablespoons chopped fresh coriander leaves
1 tablespoon chopped fresh mint
½ cucumber, diced

for the pancakes:
175 g / 6 oz plain flour
3 eggs
300 ml / 12 fl oz semi-skimmed milk
2 fresh chillies (1 red and 1 green), chopped
1 teaspoon ground pomegranate seeds
½ teaspoon ground cumin seeds
1 teaspoon chopped fresh coriander leaves
1 tablespoon low-fat margarine

1 Prepare all the vegetables and set aside on a heatproof dish. Preheat the grill.

2 Heat the oil in a small saucepan and start by adding the fenugreek leaves, the curry leaves, the crushed dried red chillies and a little salt. Stir-fry over a moderate heat for about 1 minute. Set aside.

3 Brush the vegetables with the seasoned oil and grill for 12-15 minutes. Remove from the heat.

4 Now make the raita: whisk the yoghurt using a small fork. Stir in the honey, followed by the remaining ingredients. Set aside in a serving bowl.

5 Make the pancakes: sift the flour together with a large pinch of salt into a large bowl. Beat the eggs really well, then add them to the flour. Continue beating and gradually stir in the milk.

6 Add the chillies, followed by the pomegranate seeds, cumin and coriander. Blend together well and let the batter stand for about 30 minutes.

7 Heat about ½ teaspoon of the low-fat margarine in a 25-cm / 10-inch non-stick frying pan over a moderate heat. Pour in about one-quarter of the pancake batter, tilting the pan so the batter spreads well and coats the bottom of the pan evenly.

8 When you see fine bubbles begin to appear on top of the pancake, flip it over with a spatula and cook for a minute or so on the other side. Transfer the cooked pancake to a plate and keep warm. Cook the remaining pancakes in the same way.

9 Roll up some of the vegetables in each of the pancakes and serve with the remaining vegetables and the raita.

Grilled Vegetables in a Pancake Roll

BAKED TOMATOES STUFFED WITH PANIR CUBES AND VEGETABLES

Panir is a cheese used very widely in Indian cooking, and makes a good source of protein for strict vegetarians. This cheese is available from some high-street supermarkets, but is more readily available at Indian/Pakistani grocers or can be prepared at home (page 140). Serve the stuffed tomatoes on a bed of boiled rice, with a dhal.

SERVES 4

PREPARATION
about 30 minutes
COOKING
15-20 minutes

Calories per serving *244*
Total fat *High*
Saturated fat *High*
Protein *Medium*
Carbohydrate *Low*
Cholesterol per serving
18 mg
Vitamins *A, B group, C, E*
Minerals *Calcium, Potassium, Iron, Zinc, Iodine*

4 large or beef tomatoes
60 g / 2 oz panir (see page 140)
2 tablespoons corn oil, plus more for the dish
2 tablespoons tomato purée
1 teaspoon ginger pulp (page 17)
1 teaspoon garlic pulp (page 17)
1 teaspoon ground coriander
1 teaspoon ground cumin
salt

1 teaspoon chilli powder
1 tablespoon low-fat crème fraîche
4 curry leaves
¼ teaspoon mixed onion seeds and mustard seeds
60 g / 2 oz shelled peas
½ orange or red pepper, deseeded and diced
60 g / 2 oz cauliflower, cut into small florets
1 tablespoon chopped fresh coriander leaves

1   Using a sharp knife, cut the tops off the tomatoes. With a grapefruit knife, scoop out most of the flesh. Place the hollowed-out tomatoes in a lightly greased ovenproof dish.

2   Cut the panir into 1-cm/½-inch cubes. Preheat the oven to 190°C/375°F/gas 5.

3   In a bowl, mix together the tomato purée, ginger, garlic, ground coriander, ground cumin, salt to taste, chilli powder and crème fraîche with 3 tablespoons of water.

4   Heat the oil in a kadahi, wok or deep frying pan and add the curry leaves, and the onion and mustard seeds. Fry these for about 20-30 seconds over moderate heat, then add the tomato purée mixture. Stir-fry this for about 3 minutes.

5   Add the peas, pepper, cauliflower and fresh coriander. Cook, stirring, for about 3 minutes, then add the panir cubes. Cook for 2-3 minutes more, or until the mixture is semi-dry.

6   Remove from the heat and spoon the mixture into the tomatoes, then cover with the cut tops. Bake the tomatoes in the oven for 7-10 minutes.

Baked Tomatoes Stuffed with Panir Cubes and Vegetables

BOILED EGG CURRY

SERVES 4

PREPARATION
about 15 minutes
COOKING
10-12 minutes,
plus cooking the eggs

Calories per serving *194*
Total fat *High*
Saturated fat *High*
Protein *Medium*
Carbohydrate *Low*
Cholesterol per serving
193 mg
Vitamins *A, B₂, B₃, B₁₂,*
Folate, E
Minerals *Potassium, Iron,*
Zinc, Iodine

This curry consists of a thick creamy sauce poured over hard-boiled eggs, and is delicious served with plain boiled rice with saffron.

4 hard-boiled eggs
2 tablespoons tomato purée
1 tablespoon ground coriander
large pinch of ground cardamom seeds
1 teaspoon ginger pulp (page 17)
1 teaspoon garlic pulp (page 17)

1 tablespoon ground almonds
1 tablespoon powdered coconut
1 teaspoon chilli powder
2 tablespoons sunflower oil
2 fresh green chillies, chopped
2 tablespoons chopped fresh coriander leaves

1 Shell the eggs and cut them in half lengthwise. Arrange the egg halves on a serving plate.

2 Make a paste in a bowl by mixing the tomato purée, ground coriander, cardamom, ginger, garlic, almonds, and the coconut and chilli powders. Blend together and stir in 300 ml / ½ pint water.

3 Heat the oil in a kadahi, wok or deep frying pan over moderate heat. Pour in the spice mixture, lower the heat and cook gently, stirring from time to time, for 5-7 minutes, lowering the heat further if necessary.

4 Add the fresh chillies and fresh coriander, and cook for 2 minutes more. Remove from the heat.

5 Pour the sauce over the eggs to serve.

SPICY SPINACH AND POTATO BAKE

SERVES 4

PREPARATION
about 30 minutes
COOKING
15-20 minutes

Calories per serving *224*
Total fat *High*
Saturated fat *Medium*
Protein *Medium*
Carbohydrate *Low*
Cholesterol per serving
10 mg
Vitamins *A, B group, C, E*
Minerals *Calcium,*
Potassium, Iron, Zinc

Spinach is one of my favourite vegetables. I am happy to say that most good supermarkets now sell excellent ready-washed small fresh spinach leaves, which can be used raw in salads, or lightly blanched, or cooked in this way.

450 g / 1 lb fresh spinach leaves
2 large potatoes
salt
2 tablespoons sunflower oil
1 teaspoon mixed crushed coriander seeds,
mustard seeds, white cumin seeds,
fennel seeds, onion seeds
4 curry leaves

1 onion, sliced
1 teaspoon chilli powder
1 teaspoon ginger pulp (page 17)
1 teaspoon garlic pulp (page 17)
1 medium red pepper, deseeded and sliced
1 tablespoon fresh coriander leaves
60 g / 2 oz mozzarella cheese, grated

1 Unless you buy the ready-prepared type, wash the spinach thoroughly and cut off any extra-long stalks. Peel the potatoes and cut them into slices.

2 Blanch the spinach in boiling salted water for about 2 minutes. Drain, placing the spinach in a sieve to get rid of any excess water, and set aside.

3 Preheat a hot grill. Heat the oil in a heavy-based pan, throw in the mixed seeds and fry over moderate heat for about 30 seconds. Add the curry leaves and onion. Fry until the onion is soft and golden.

4 Reduce heat and add the chilli powder, ginger, garlic and salt to taste. Stir-fry for 30 seconds, then add the potato and stir gently for a minute or so.

5 Next add the sliced red pepper and the spinach, cover the pan with a lid and cook over a low heat for 7-10 minutes, checking and stirring at least once. Try not to break the potato slices.

6 Once the potatoes are tender, transfer the contents of the pan to a heatproof dish and sprinkle with the fresh coriander and the mozzarella. Place under the hot grill and grill until the cheese has melted and is slightly browned. Serve immediately.

DOODHI WITH MOONG DHAL

450 g / 1 lb doodhi (page 20) or other pumpkin
1 cup of moong dhal (yellow split mung beans, page 23)
1½ tablespoons corn oil
½ teaspoon mixed fennel seeds, crushed coriander seeds and white cumin seeds
1 onion, sliced
1 teaspoon ginger pulp (page 17)
1 teaspoon chilli powder
1 teaspoon garlic pulp (page 17)
salt
2 green chillies, slit in the middle
2 red chillies, slit in the middle
1 tablespoon fresh coriander leaves, to garnish

SERVES 4

PREPARATION
about 20 minutes
COOKING
about 35 minutes

Calories per serving *193*
Total fat *Medium*
Saturated fat *Low*
Protein *High*
Carbohydrate *Medium*
Cholesterol per serving *None*
Vitamins A, B₁. B₃, Folate, C, E
Minerals *Potassium, Iron, Zinc*

1 Peel the doodhi and cut it into small pieces. Bring about 850 ml / 1½ pints of salted water to the boil and drop in the doodhi. Boil for about 5 minutes. Drain the water and set the doodhi aside.

2 Wash and pick over the moong dhal for any stones, etc. Place in a heavy-based pan and cover generously with water. Bring to the boil and cook for about 15 minutes over a medium heat, stirring occasionally (a spoon in the pan prevents it boiling over), until soft but not mushy. Drain and set aside.

3 Heat the oil in a large heavy-based pan and fry the mixed seeds for 30 seconds over a moderate heat. Add the onions and stir-fry for 3 minutes.

4 Add the ginger, chilli powder, garlic and salt to taste. Next add the lentils and doodhi pieces, and gently stir using a wooden spoon.

5 Drop in the chillies and pour in 150 ml / ¼ pint of water. Lower the heat, cover the pan and cook for 3-5 minutes.

6 Serve garnished with the fresh coriander leaves.

Overleaf: Doodhi with Moong Dhal, Spicy Spinach and Potato Bake

POTATOES IN A SOUR SAUCE

SERVES 4

This curry is traditionally made with lamb and potatoes, but this vegetarian equivalent is equally delicious.

PREPARATION
about 25 minutes
COOKING
20-25 minutes

Calories per serving *469*
Total fat *Low*
Saturated fat *Low*
Protein *Low*
Carbohydrate *High*
Cholesterol per serving
None
Vitamins *B₁, B₃, B₆, Folate,*
C, E
Minerals *Calcium,*
Potassium, Iron, Zinc,
Selenium, Iodine

15 baby potatoes
1 tablespoon lemon juice
1 teaspoon tamarind paste
1 teaspoon sugar
1½ teaspoon ground coriander
½ teaspoon chilli powder
1 teaspoon garlic pulp (page 17)
1 teaspoon ginger pulp (page 17)

salt
1 tablespoon oil
4 curry leaves
3 onions, finely chopped
1 green pepper, deseeded and coarsely chopped
1 tablespoon chopped fresh mint
1 tablespoon chopped fresh coriander leaves

1 Boil the potatoes until soft but not mushy. Drain and, when cool enough to handle, cut them in half and set aside.

2 In a bowl, blend together the lemon juice, tamarind, sugar, ground coriander, chilli powder, garlic, ginger and salt to taste. Mix to a paste with about 300 ml / ½ pint water and set aside.

3 Heat the oil in a heavy-based saucepan and fry the curry leaves with the onions for about 2 minutes over moderate heat, stirring very occasionally. Pour the spice mixture over the top of the onions and let this cook for 2-3 minutes.

4 Next add the potatoes, mixing them in gently. Cover and cook for a further 5-7 minutes. Remove the lid and stir gently. The sauce should be quite thick by this time.

5 Now add the green pepper, the mint and the fresh coriander. Mix it in and serve hot.

CHANA DHAL WITH PANIR AND TOMATOES

This dhal has a crunchy texture and the tomatoes and panir make it look very attractive. It is delicious served simply, with an accompaniment of plain boiled rice.

SERVES 4

PREPARATION
about 15 minutes
COOKING
about 20 minutes

175 g / 6 oz chana dhal (page 23)
1 onion, diced
1 teaspoon garam masala
1 teaspoon garlic pulp (page 17)
1 teaspoon ginger pulp (page 17)
½ teaspoon chilli powder
½ teaspoon mango powder
salt
chopped fresh coriander leaves, to garnish

for the tarka (seasoned oil):
1 tablespoon corn oil
½ teaspoon white cumin seeds
4 curry leaves
3 whole garlic cloves
6 whole baby onions, peeled
6 bite-sized cubes of panir (page 140)
6 whole cherry tomatoes

1   Wash and pick over the chana dhal or split peas for any stones, etc. Place them in a heavy-based saucepan with the onion, garam masala, garlic, ginger, chilli powder, mango powder, salt and about 600 ml / 1 pint water. Bring to the boil and cook for about 15 minutes over a medium heat, stirring occasionally (put a spoon in the pan to prevent it from boiling over).

2   Meanwhile, prepare the tarka by heating the oil and frying the cumin seeds, curry leaves, garlic cloves, baby onions, panir cubes and cherry tomatoes. Because there is very little oil in this you will need to shake the pan continuously to prevent the whole spices from burning.

3   Once the dhal is cooked and the water is almost absorbed, pour the tarka over the lentils and mix everything into the dhal.

4   Serve sprinkled with the chopped coriander.

Calories per serving *274*
Total fat *Medium*
Saturated fat *Low*
Protein *High*
Carbohydrate *Medium*
Cholesterol per serving *15 mg*
Vitamins A, *B group, C, E*
Minerals *Calcium, Potassium, Iron, Zinc, Iodine*

CAULIFLOWER WITH PEPPERS

Try to choose smaller cauliflowers, even if it means you need to buy two, as these are usually fresher-looking and also firmer and easier to manage. This very colourful vegetarian curry is best eaten with freshly made chapati.

1 medium cauliflower (or 2 small, see above)
8 baby potatoes
1 red pepper
1 yellow pepper
60 g / 2 oz shelled peas
1 tablespoon corn oil
¼ teaspoon white cumin seeds
6 curry leaves
3 whole dried red chillies

2 onions, sliced
3 garlic cloves, chopped
2 teaspoons shredded ginger
1 teaspoon chilli powder
¼ teaspoon turmeric
salt
1 tablespoon chopped fresh coriander leaves, to garnish

SERVES 4

PREPARATION
about 20 minutes
COOKING
12-15 minutes

1   Cut the cauliflower into small florets; cut the potatoes into slices; deseed the peppers and cut them into strips.

2   Pour the oil into a heavy-based saucepan set over a moderate heat and add the cumin seeds, curry leaves and the whole red chillies. Quickly move them around to prevent burning.

3   Add the sliced onions, garlic and ginger. Continue to cook for about 2 minutes, still stirring frequently to prevent the onions from burning.

4   Add all the prepared vegetables, followed by the chilli powder, turmeric and salt to taste. Blend everything together and cover. Lower the heat and cook for 5-7 minutes. The steam should cook the vegetables. However, if you feel the dish is getting very dry, add about 150 ml / ¼ pint of water.

5   Served garnished with the fresh coriander.

Calories per serving *185*
Total fat *Low*
Saturated fat *Low*
Protein *Medium*
Carbohydrate *High*
Cholesterol per serving *None*
Vitamins A, B_1, B_3. B_6, *Folate, C, E*
Minerals Potassium, Iron, Zinc

SWEETCORN AND PEAS WITH PANIR

SERVES 4

This quick stir-fry makes a good side dish, or even a main course served with freshly made chapati *(see page 124).*

PREPARATION
about 10 minutes
COOKING
12-15 minutes

Calories per serving *145*
Total fat *Medium*
Saturated fat *Low*
Protein *Medium*
Carbohydrate *Medium*
Cholesterol per serving
None
Vitamins *A, B₁, B₃,B₆,*
Folate, C, E
Minerals *Potassium, Iron,*
Zinc

225 g / 8 oz sweetcorn kernels
125 g / 4½ oz shelled peas
10-12 cubes of panir (page 140)
1 large carrot
½ red pepper
1 tablespoon corn oil
2 onions, finely chopped

2.5-cm / 1-inch piece of ginger, grated
2 garlic cloves, finely chopped
1½ teaspoons crushed dried red chillies
salt
fresh mint leaves, for garnish
sprigs of fresh coriander, for garnish

1 Chop the carrot. Deseed the red pepper and slice it.

2 Heat the oil and fry the onion for 2-3 minutes, stirring occasionally. Add the sweetcorn, peas, chopped carrot and pepper slices, followed by the ginger, garlic, crushed chillies and salt to taste. Continue to stir-fry over a moderate heat for 3-5 minutes.

3 Add the panir and cook for 3-5 minutes more.

4 Serve garnished with the mint and coriander.

BAY RICE WITH PEAS

SERVES 4

Rice and peas are cooked together in several different ways, and always make a good combination. This particular dish is delicately flavoured with bay and some other whole spices.

PREPARATION
about 10 minutes
COOKING
20-25 minutes,
plus 5 minutes'
standing

Calories per serving *268*
Total fat *Low*
Saturated fat *Low*
Protein *Low*
Carbohydrate *High*
Cholesterol per serving
None
Vitamins *B₃, Folate, E*
Minerals *Iron, Potassium*

2 cups of basmati rice
85 g / 3 oz shelled peas
1 tablespoon each olive and corn oil
1 onion, sliced
1 teaspoon ginger pulp (page 17)
1 teaspoon garlic pulp (page 17)

salt
1 bay leaf
3 whole cloves
1 small piece of cinnamon stick
6-8 black peppercorns
2 whole black cardamoms

1 Wash the rice well and place it in a bowl.

2 Heat the olive oil and corn oil together in a large heavy-based saucepan and fry the onion over a moderate heat until golden brown. Add the ginger, garlic, salt to taste, the bay leaf, cloves, cinnamon, black peppercorns and cardamoms. Cook for about 30 seconds.

3 Add the rice, stirring it in gently so you do not damage it. Add the peas. Pour in 3 cups of water and bring to the boil. Lower the heat, cover the pan and cook for 10-15 minutes.

4 Let the rice rest off the heat, but still covered, for 5 minutes before serving. If you prefer, remove the cinnamon and cloves before serving.

Sweetcorn and Peas with Panir

SPINACH WITH GARLIC AND FROMAGE FRAIS

SERVES 4

PREPARATION
about 15 minutes
COOKING
10-15 minutes

Calories per serving *87*
Total fat *High*
Saturated fat *Medium*
Protein *High*
Carbohydrate *Low*
Cholesterol per serving
3 mg
Vitamins *A, B group, C, E*
Minerals *Calcium,
Potassium, Iron, Zinc*

750 g / 1½ lb fresh spinach leaves, chopped
salt
1 tablespoon olive oil
2.5-cm / 1-inch piece of cinnamon stick
2 whole cloves

3 garlic cloves, coarsely chopped
2 fresh red chillies, chopped
2 tablespoons chopped fresh coriander leaves
2 tablespoons virtually fat-free fromage frais

1 Wash the spinach thoroughly, unless it is ready prepared, and blanch it in boiling salted water for 2 minutes. Drain the spinach in a sieve and leave to let as much water run off as possible.

2 Heat the olive oil in a kadahi, wok or deep frying pan over a low heat and add the cinnamon, cloves, garlic, 1 of the chopped chillies, followed by the spinach. Quickly stir-fry over a moderate heat.

3 Add salt to taste, the fresh coriander and the remaining red chillies and continue to stir-fry for a further 2-3 minutes over a low heat.

4 Stir in the fromage frais and cook for 1-1½ minutes more. If you prefer, remove the cinnamon and cloves before serving.

SPICY RICE AND VEGETABLE STIR-FRY

SERVES 4

PREPARATION
about 20 minutes
COOKING
*30-35 minutes,
plus 5 minutes'
standing*

Calories per serving *338*
Total fat *Low*
Saturated fat *Low*
Protein *Low*
Carbohydrate *High*
Cholesterol per serving
None
Vitamins *A, B₁, B₃, B₆,
Folate, C, E*
Minerals *Potassium, Iron*

2 cups of basmati rice
2 tablespoons corn oil
6 curry leaves
*½ teaspoon mixed onion seeds, mustard seeds,
cumin seeds and fenugreek seeds*
1 teaspoon garlic pulp (page 17)
1 teaspoon ginger pulp (page 17)
1 onion, chopped
2 tomatoes, sliced

60 g / 2 oz sweetcorn kernels
60 g / 2 oz peas
60 g/ 2 oz green beans, cut into pieces
1 carrot, diced
salt
2 tablespoons lemon juice
2 tablespoons chopped fresh coriander leaves
2 green chillies, diced
sliced hard-boiled egg, to garnish (optional)

1 Rinse the rice until the water runs clear and leave it to soak while you prepare the vegetables.

2 Heat the oil in a large heavy-based saucepan. Fry the curry leaves and seeds for about 45 seconds. Lower the heat and add the garlic ginger and onion. Stir-fry for about 3 minutes.

3 Start adding all the other vegetables, beginning with the tomatoes and stir-fry each for about 2 minutes before adding the next vegetable.

4 Add the lemon juice, coriander and chillies with salt to taste. Drain the rice well, add it to the vegetables and stir-fry for a further minute. Add 3 cups of water and bring to the boil. Reduce the heat to medium-low, cover and cook for 10-15 minutes.

6 Let stand, covered, for 5 minutes off the heat before serving. Garnish with egg slices, if you like.

Spinach with Garlic and Fromage Frais

Rice and Breads

NAAN
Yeasted Bread

There are many ways of making naan, *but this particular recipe is very easy to follow.* Naan *should be served warm, preferably as soon as they are cooked. If you aren't too concerned about calories and fat content, and want a more authentic* naan, *use butter rather than the olive oil.*

MAKES 6

PREPARATION
*about 25 minutes,
plus 3-4 hours'
rising*
COOKING
15-20 minutes

Calories per serving *350*
Total fat *Medium*
Saturated fat *Medium*
Protein *Low*
Carbohydrate *Medium*
Cholesterol per serving
11 mg
Vitamins *A, B₁, B₃, B₆,
Folate*
Minerals *Calcium, Iron,
Iodine, Potassium*

1 teaspoon sugar
1 teaspoon fresh yeast
225 g / 8 oz plain flour, plus more for dusting
1 tablespoon ghee or melted butter
1 teaspoon salt
4 tablespoons olive oil
1 teaspoon sesame seeds or poppy seeds
corn oil, for brushing the foil

1   Put the sugar and yeast in a cup with 150 ml / ¼ pint warm warm water. Mix well until the yeast has dissolved and leave for 10 minutes, or until frothy.

2   Place the flour in a large mixing bowl. Make a well in the middle, add the ghee or butter and salt and pour in the yeast mixture. Mix well, using your hands and adding a little more water if required to achieve a soft and pliable dough.

3   Turn the dough out on a floured surface and knead for about 5 minutes or until smooth.

4   Place the dough back in the bowl, cover and leave to rise in a warm place for 3-4 hours, or until doubled in size.

5   Preheat a very hot grill and line the grill pan with foil. Grease the foil lightly with corn oil.

6   Turn the dough out on a floured surface and knead it for a further 2 minutes. Break it into 6 small balls with your hand and pat these into rounds about 12.5 cm / 5 inches in diameter and about 1 cm / ½ inch thick.

7   Place 2 or 3 of the rounds in the grill pan, brush with some of the olive oil and sprinkle with sesame seeds or poppy seeds. Grill under the preheated grill for 7-10 minutes, turning twice, brushing with olive oil and sprinkling with sesame or poppy seeds each time until golden and lightly puffed up. Wrap the naan in foil to keep warm, while you cook the rest.

CHAPATI
Unleavened Bread

This is one of the healthiest of Indian breads, because it contains no fat. However, some people like to brush it with a little melted butter before serving. Ideally chapati *should be eaten as they come off the* thawa *(a slightly concave circular cast-iron plate or skillet) or out of the frying pan; if that is not practical, however, keep them warm after cooking by wrapping them in foil. In India,* chapati *are sometimes cooked on a naked flame, which makes them puff up. Allow about 2 per person.*

Previous pages: Chapati and Naan

225 g / 8 oz wholemeal ata or chapati flour (see page 28), plus more for dusting

½ teaspoon salt

MAKES 8-12

PREPARATION
15-20 minutes, plus 15-20 minutes resting (optional)
COOKING
30-40 minutes

Calories per serving *208*
Total fat *Low*
Saturated fat *Low*
Protein *Low*
Carbohydrate *High*
Cholesterol per serving *None*
Vitamins *B₁, B₃*
Minerals *Potassium, Iron, Zinc*

1 Place the flour in a mixing bowl with the salt. Make a well in the middle of the flour and gradually stir in 200 ml / 7 fl oz of water, mixing well with your fingers to form a supple dough.

2 Knead the dough for about 7-10 minutes until it is soft and pliable. Ideally, leave it to rest for about 15-20 minutes; if time is short, however, roll it out immediately.

3 Divide the dough into 8-12 roughly equal portions. Roll out each piece on a well-floured surface. Have some foil ready in which to wrap the cooked chapati in to keep them warm.

4 Place a heavy-based frying pan or a thawa over a high heat. When it is almost smoking hot, lower the heat to moderate. Place a chapati in the pan and, when it bubbles, turn it over. Press it down with a clean tea-cloth or a flat spoon and turn once again when small patches of brown start to appear on the underside and it begins to puff up.

5 Remove from the pan and keep warm. Repeat the process until all the chapati are cooked.

ROTI
Gram Flour Bread

MAKES 8-10

PREPARATION
about 20 minutes, plus 5-7 minutes' resting
COOKING
15-20 minutes

Calories per serving *112*
Total fat *Medium*
Saturated fat *Low*
Protein *Low*
Carbohydrate *Low*
Cholesterol per serving *None*
Vitamins *B₁, B₃, B₆, Folate, E*
Minerals *Potassium, Iron, Zinc, Selenium*

115 g / 4 oz wholemeal flour, plus more for dusting
115 g / 4 oz gram flour (page 29)
1 tablespoon chopped fresh coriander leaves
1 fresh red chilli, deseeded and chopped

1 small onion, finely diced
¼ teaspoon onion seeds
large pinch of salt
3-4 tablespoons corn oil

1 Sift both the flours into a mixing bowl. Add the coriander, chilli, onion, onion seeds and salt. Using a fork, blend everything together. Gradually pour in about 200 ml / 7 fl oz water, just enough to form a soft pliable dough. Knead on a floured surface for 45 seconds, then let rest for about 5-7 minutes.

2 Divide the dough into 8-10 balls and, on a well-floured surface, roll each into a 12.5-15-cm / 5-6-inch round.

3 Heat a thawa or non-stick frying pan over a high heat and, when very hot, turn the heat down slightly. Place a dough round on the pan and, after 30 seconds, sprinkle 1 teaspoon of oil over it and turn it over. Cook, moving the roti around on the pan, and turn it over again. It will puff up, so press it down with a spatula to ensure even cooking. When well browned on both sides, remove and keep warm, wrapped in foil, while cooking the rest.

AROMATIC RICE WITH PEAS

I have made plain boiled rice just a little more interesting by adding some whole spices and peas.

2 cups of basmati rice
85 g / 3 oz shelled peas
2 cardamom pods
¼ teaspoon black cumin seeds
1 cinnamon stick

4 black peppercorns
1 fresh bay leaf
½ teaspoon salt
fried sliced onions for garnish (optional)

1 Rinse the rice thoroughly and gently until the water runs clear.

2 Pour 3 cups of water into a large saucepan and add the whole spices, followed by the salt. Place the saucepan over a high heat and when the water begins to boil, lower the heat and throw in the rice and peas. Cover the pan with a lid and cook over a medium heat for 12-15 minutes, or until all the water has been absorbed and the rice is cooked.

3 Let the rice stand off the heat, covered, for 5 minutes and serve using a slotted spoon to prevent the rice becoming mushy. Garnish with fried onion if you like.

TAMATAR AUR MATAR KAY CHAWAL
Tomato and Pea Rice

2 cups of basmati rice
2 tomatoes, sliced
60 g / 2 oz shelled peas
2 tablespoons corn oil
1 medium onion, sliced

large pinch of onion seeds
6-8 curry leaves
½ teaspoon ginger pulp (page 17)
½ teaspoon garlic pulp (page 17)
salt

1 Rinse the rice thoroughly until the water runs clear. Leave it to soak in fresh water while you do the rest of the preparation.

2 Heat the oil in a large heavy-based saucepan over moderate heat. Add the onion, onion seeds and curry leaves, and fry for about 5 minutes, stirring frequently, until the onion is soft and golden.

3 Add the ginger, garlic, tomato and salt to taste. Stir-fry for another 3 minutes.

4 Add the rice and stir gently for about 1 minute, then add 3 cups of water and the peas. Bring to the boil, then lower the heat, cover the pan tightly and simmer gently for about 10-15 minutes, until all the water is absorbed and the rice is tender.

Aromatic Rice with Peas

RICE WITH PINE NUTS

This is an excellent and versatile rice dish. I really enjoy it with the Lemon and Garlic Plaice on page 49.

on page 49.

SERVES 4

PREPARATION
10 minutes
COOKING
*20-25 minutes,
plus 5 minutes
standing*

Calories per serving *306*
Total fat *Medium*
Saturated fat *Low*
Protein *Low*
Carbohydrate *High*
Cholesterol per serving
None
Vitamins *B₃, E*
Minerals *Potassium, Iron*

2 cups of basmati rice
1 tablespoon corn oil
¼ teaspoon mustard seeds
4 curry leaves

½ teaspoon ginger pulp (page 17)
½ teaspoon garlic pulp (page 17)
½ teaspoon salt
30 g / 1 oz pine nuts

1   Rinse the rice thoroughly until the water runs clear. Leave to soak in fresh water.

2   Heat the oil in a large heavy-based saucepan. Add the mustard seeds and the curry leaves and fry for about 40 seconds. Lower the heat and add the ginger, garlic, salt and pine nuts. Stir-fry for a further 30 seconds.

3   Drain the water from the rice and pour the rice into the pan. Continue to stir-fry for another 30 seconds, then pour in 3 cups of fresh water. Bring to the boil, then reduce the heat to moderate. Cover the pan and cook for 10-15 minutes.

4   Leave to stand off the heat, covered, for 5-7 minutes before serving.

RICE WITH DESICCATED COCONUT

This tasty way with rice can be served with any of the dishes from this book.

SERVES 4

PREPARATION
about 20 minutes
COOKING
*24-30 minutes,
plus 5 minutes'
standing*

Calories per serving *322*
Total fat *Low*
Saturated fat *Low*
Protein *Low*
Carbohydrate *High*
Cholesterol per serving
None
Vitamins *A, B₃, B₆, C, E*
Minerals *Potassium, Iron*

2 cups of basmati rice
1 tablespoon corn oil
4-6 curry leaves
large pinch of onion seeds
1 medium onion, sliced
2 garlic cloves, sliced

1 teaspoon shredded ginger
salt
1 large carrot, diced
2 tablespoons desiccated coconut
1 tablespoon chopped fresh coriander leaves
1 red chilli, chopped

1   Rinse the rice until the water runs clear. Leave to soak in fresh water.

2   Meanwhile, in a large heavy-based saucepan, heat the oil and stir-fry the curry leaves, onion seeds and the onion for 2 minutes.

3   Next add the garlic, ginger, salt to taste, carrots, half the desiccated coconut and half the fresh coriander. Stir to mix everything.

4   Next, drain the water from the rice and add the rice to the pan. Stir-fry gently for about 1 minute.

5   Add the remaining desiccated coconut and fresh coriander, and the chopped chilli, followed by 3 cups of water. Bring to the boil, lower the heat to moderate, cover and cook for 10-15 minutes, until the rice is just tender.

6   Let the rice stand off the heat, covered, for about 5 minutes before serving.

SAFFRON RICE MOULDS

2 cups of basmati rice
1 tablespoon olive oil
1 tablespoon corn oil, plus more for the moulds
2 black cardamom pods
large pinch of black cumin seeds
6 black peppercorns

2 cloves
salt
½ teaspoon saffron threads
2 tablespoons sultanas
1 tablespoon flaked almonds

SERVES 4

PREPARATION
10 minutes
COOKING
*about 30 minutes,
plus 5-7 minutes
standing*

Calories per serving *295*
Total fat *Medium*
Saturated fat *Low*
Protein *Low*
Carbohydrate *High*
Cholesterol per serving *None*
Vitamins *E*
Minerals *Potassium, Iron*

1 Rinse the rice thoroughly until the water runs clear. Leave it to soak in fresh water while preparing the rest of the ingredients.

2 In a large heavy-based saucepan, heat the oils together over moderate heat for about 30 seconds, then add the cardamom pods, cumin seeds, peppercorns, cloves and salt to taste. Lower the heat and stir.

3 Drain the rice, add to the pan and stir gently. Add the saffron, sultanas, almonds and 3 cups of water. Bring to the boil, lower the heat, cover and cook for 10-15 minutes, until the water is fully absorbed and the rice is tender. Let stand, off the heat, still covered, for 5-7 minutes.

4 While the rice is cooking, preheat the oven to 190°C/375°F/gas 5 and lightly grease 4 ramekins with corn oil. Press the rice into them and warm through in the oven for about 5-10 minutes.

5 Carefully unmould the rice to serve.

Salads, Side Dishes and Accompaniments

TOMATO AND ONION SALAD

SERVES 4

Versions of this versatile fresh-tasting salad are served at most dinner tables in Indian and Pakistani homes.

PREPARATION
about 15 minutes

Calories per serving *39*
Total fat *Low*
Saturated fat *Low*
Protein *Low*
Carbohydrate *High*
Cholesterol per serving
None
Vitamins *A, B₁, B₃, B₆,*
Folate, C, E
Minerals *Potassium*

1 red onion, diced
2 tomatoes, diced
1 large carrot, diced
½ medium cucumber, diced
1 green chilli, deseeded and sliced

1 tablespoon chopped fresh coriander
**1 tablespoon chopped fresh mint, plus some sprigs
to garnish (optional)**
salt
2 tablespoons lime juice

1 Put the diced onion, tomatoes, carrot and cucumber in a salad bowl. Add the chilli and herbs with salt to taste.

2 Using a fork, gently mix everything together.
3 Sprinkle over the lime juice and, if you wish, garnish with sprigs of mint to serve.

BOMBAY POTATOES

SERVES 4

Bombay potatoes, given a sweet-and-sour flavour by the addition of sugar and tamarind paste, make a delicious accompaniment to almost any dish.

PREPARATION
about 15 minutes
COOKING
15-20 minutes

Calories per serving *222*
Total fat *Medium*
Saturated fat *Low*
Protein *Low*
Carbohydrate *High*
Cholesterol per serving
None
Vitamins *B₁, B₃, B₆, Folate,*
C, E
Minerals *Potassium, Iron,*
Iodine

15 baby potatoes, scrubbed and halved
salt
2 tablespoons tomato purée
2 tablespoons tomato ketchup
1 tablespoon tamarind paste
1 teaspoon sugar
1 teaspoon ginger pulp (page 17)
1½ teaspoons ground coriander

1 teaspoon garlic pulp (page 17)
1 teaspoon chilli powder
1 tablespoon lemon juice
2 tablespoons corn oil
¼ teaspoon onion seeds
6 curry leaves
1 tablespoon finely chopped fresh coriander leaves
1 large fresh green chilli, chopped

1 Cook the baby potatoes in boiling salted water until just tender. Drain and set aside.
2 Meanwhile, in a bowl mix the tomato purée, tomato ketchup, tamarind paste, sugar, ginger, ground coriander, garlic, chilli powder and lemon juice with salt to taste and 225 ml / 8 fl oz water.

3 In a heavy-based saucepan over a moderate heat, heat the oil with the onion seeds and curry leaves. Lower the heat and add the tomato paste. Quickly stir-fry for about 1 minute, then add the potatoes. Continue to stir-fry for a further 2 minutes.
4 Stir in the fresh coriander and chillies and serve.

Previous pages: Bombay Potatoes, Mango and Apple Chutney (page 139) and Tomato and Onion Salad

MIXED SALAD WITH SWEETCORN

Although not traditional, this salad, with its garlic-flavoured dressing, has a nice, slightly spicy tang.

3 whole radicchio leaves
6 whole leaves from an iceberg lettuce
1 celery stalk, sliced
1 spring onion, chopped
½ cucumber, sliced
1 medium-sized cooked beetroot, diced
**60 g / 2 oz fresh cooked or defrosted frozen
sweetcorn kernels**
60 g / 2 oz fresh baby peas
6 cherry tomatoes (preferably with their stalks)

for the dressing :
1 tablespoon olive oil
½ teaspoon crushed dried red chillies
1 tablespoon lemon juice
2 garlic cloves, crushed
1 teaspoon caster sugar
salt
¼ teaspoon freshly ground black pepper
1 tablespoon very finely chopped fresh coriander

1 Line a salad bowl with the radicchio and iceberg lettuce leaves. Sprinkle the celery, spring onion and cucumber over the top. Make a circle around the edge with the diced beetroot.

2 Mix together the sweetcorn and peas and arrange them in the centre of the salad. Arrange the cherry tomatoes all around the salad.

3 Make the dressing: place the olive oil in a small bowl with the red chillies, lemon juice, crushed garlic, sugar, salt to taste, black pepper and fresh coriander. Mix well with a spoon and pour all over the salad to serve.

SERVES 4

PREPARATION
about 20 minutes

Calories per serving *77*
Total fat *High*
Saturated fat *Low*
Protein *Low*
Carbohydrate *Low*
Cholesterol per serving
None
Vitamins *B₁, B₃, B₆, Folate,
C, E*
Minerals *Potassium, Iron*

SPICY POTATO AND KIDNEY BEAN SALAD

6-8 baby potatoes
salt
60 g / 2 oz plain low-fat runny yoghurt
225 g / 8 oz virtually fat-free fromage frais
1 garlic clove, finely chopped
1 teaspoon crushed dried red chillies
1 teaspoon sugar

1 tablespoon lime juice
2 tablespoons chopped fresh coriander leaves
½ red pepper, deseeded and diced
1 tablespoon chopped fresh mint
60 g / 2 oz canned red kidney beans, drained
1 spring onion, chopped, to garnish

1 Scrub the potatoes, halve them and boil them in salted water until soft but not mushy. Remove from the heat and leave in the water, covered.

2 In a bowl, whisk together the yoghurt, fromage frais and garlic. Gradually add salt to taste, the crushed red chillies, sugar, lime juice and coriander.

Mix everything together well and set aside.

3 Drain the potatoes and add them to the yoghurt sauce, followed by the red pepper, mint and beans. Mix together well.

4 Transfer to a serving dish and serve garnished with the chopped spring onion.

SERVES 4

PREPARATION
about 20 minutes
COOKING
about 15 minutes

Calories per serving *130*
Total fat *Low*
Saturated fat *Low*
Protein *Medium*
Carbohydrate *High*
Cholesterol per serving
2 mg
Vitamins *A, B group, C*
Minerals *Calcium,
Potassium, Iron, Zinc,
Iodine*

CHICKPEA SALAD

SERVES 4

I recommend using canned chickpeas for this dish, as they have just the right texture .

PREPARATION
about 20 minutes
COOKING
2-3 minutes

Calories per serving *187*
Total fat *Medium*
Saturated fat *Low*
Protein *High*
Carbohydrate *Low*
Cholesterol per serving
None
Vitamins *A, B₁, B₃, B₆,*
Folate, C, E
Minerals *Calcium,*
Potassium, Iron, Zinc,
Iodine

1 400-g / 14-oz can of chickpeas
1 teaspoon cumin seeds
1 teaspoon coriander seeds
½ red sweet pepper, deseeded and diced
½ orange sweet pepper, deseeded and diced
¼ small red cabbage, shredded
1 iceberg lettuce, shredded
1 large carrot, diced
½ cucumber, sliced
½ red onion, sliced

1 teaspoon fresh coriander (optional)
1 teaspoon fresh mint (optional)

for the dressing:
2 garlic cloves, crushed
salt
1 tablespoon olive oil
2 tablespoons lemon juice
large pinch of sugar
1 teaspoon crushed dried red chillies.

1 Drain the chickpeas. Dry-roast the cumin and coriander seeds in a non-stick pan, then crush them lightly with a pestle and mortar.

2 Make the dressing: in a small bowl, mix all the ingredients and set aside.

3 Mix all the remaining salad ingredients in a salad bowl. Pour the dressing over and toss everything together to coat the salad uniformly.

4 Finally, sprinkle the cumin and coriander seeds over the top before serving.

Chickpea Salad

SPINACH AND SWEET POTATO SALAD

I love spinach, whether in a salad or cooked, and the baby spinach leaves now readily available washed and pre-packed are ideal for salads. This colourful dish also includes sweet potato, carrots, and red and green peppers. It is served with a crunchy dressing.

SERVES 4

PREPARATION
about 20 minutes
COOKING
about 25 minutes

Calories per serving *410*
Total fat *High*
Saturated fat *Low*
Protein *Medium*
Carbohydrate *Low*
Cholesterol per serving
4 mg
Vitamins *A, B group, C, E*
Minerals *Calcium,
Potassium, Iron, Zinc,
Iodine*

1 medium sweet potato
salt
1 large carrot, sliced
20-25 baby spinach leaves
1 red pepper, deseeded and sliced
½ green pepper, deseeded and diced
2 spring onions, sliced at an angle

for the dressing:
30 g / 1 oz pine nuts
30 g / 1 oz sultanas
5 walnuts
1 tablespoon chopped fresh coriander leaves
1 red chilli, chopped
1 tablespoon honey
1 tablespoon plain low-fat runny yoghurt
2 tablespoons virtually fat-free fromage frais
coarsely ground black pepper

1   Cook the sweet potato in boiling salted water until soft. Drain and slice, then set aside. Boil the carrot slices in the same way, drain and let cool.

2   On a serving plate mix the spinach leaves, sweet potato and carrot slices. Decorate with the red and green peppers and spring onion.

3   Make the dressing: in a bowl, mix together the pine nuts, sultanas and walnuts (if you like, reserve a little of each and some of the chilli for garnish). In another bowl, mix together the coriander, chilli, honey, yoghurt, fromage frais and salt to taste. Pour this over the nuts and sultanas and blend everything together. Season with coarsely ground black pepper.

4   Serve the dressing with the salad, garnished with the reserved chilli, nuts and fruit if you wish.

Spinach and Sweet Potato Salad

KACHOOMER WITH BLACK-EYE BEANS

SERVES 4

PREPARATION
about 25 minutes
COOKING
about 10 minutes

Calories per serving *39*
Total fat *Low*
Saturated fat *Low*
Protein *High*
Carbohydrate *High*
Cholesterol per serving
None
Vitamins *B₁, B₃, B₆,
Folate, C*
Minerals *Potassium, Iron*

Kachoomer is a side salad which is very popular in Indian and Pakistani meals. It is usually made with just tomatoes, onion, coriander and chillies. I like to add a few other ingredients to make it even more interesting.

2 tablespoons black-eye beans
1 red onion, finely chopped
¹/₂ cucumber, diced
2 tomatoes, sliced
2 green chillies, chopped
1 large carrot, finely grated
1 tablespoon chopped fresh mint

2 tablespoons chopped fresh coriander leaves
1 garlic clove, finely chopped
2 tablespoons lemon juice
salt
¹/₂ teaspoon coarsely ground black peppercorns
sprigs of mint, to garnish

1 Ideally the black-eye beans should be soaked overnight; however, as the quantity is very small, you can just boil them in salted water for about 10 minutes, drain off the water and set aside.

2 Place all the prepared vegetables and herbs in a serving dish with the drained black-eye beans.

Using a fork, gently mix everything together, trying not to mash any of the vegetables.

3 Finally, mix in the garlic, lemon juice, salt to taste and black pepper.

4 Serve garnished with the mint sprigs.

MANGO AND APPLE CHUTNEY

Chutneys and pickles are served at most Indian meals. Normally a helping of about 1 teaspoon of chutney is taken and put on the side of the plate. (See page 131.)

2 large mangoes
2 large green cooking apples
2 whole cloves
3.5-cm / 1½-inch length of cinnamon stick
1 teaspoon crushed dried red chillies or 1 fresh red chilli, chopped

6 tablespoons soft brown sugar
1 teaspoon garam masala
1 teaspoon shredded ginger
1 teaspoon salt
300 ml / ½ pint malt vinegar
1 tablespoon chopped fresh mint leaves

1 Peel the mangoes, remove the stones and discard them, then chop the flesh coarsely (see page 24). Peel and core the apples, and slice them coarsely. Place both the fruits in a heavy-based saucepan.

2 Add the cloves, cinnamon, chillies, sugar, garam masala, ginger, salt and malt vinegar. Stir everything together, bring to a simmer and cook over a medium heat for 10-15 minutes, or until most of the liquid has evaporated.

3 Stir in the fresh mint and cook for a further 2 minutes. Leave to cool.

4 Transfer to a sterile jar and seal. This chutney will keep in the refrigerator for up to one month.

PREPARATION
about 10 minutes
COOKING
15-20 minutes, plus cooling

Calories per serving *180*
Total fat *Low*
Saturated fat Low
Protein *Low*
Carbohydrate *High*
Cholesterol per serving *None*
Vitamins *A, B₃, B₆, Folate, C, E*
Minerals *Potassium, Iron*

SWEET-AND-SOUR CHICKPEA AND SESAME SEED CHUTNEY

115 g / 4 oz drained canned chickpeas
85 g / 3 oz sesame seeds
2 tablespoons sugar
1 tablespoon tamarind pulp
2 green chillies, coarsely chopped

2 tablespoons chopped fresh coriander
salt
4 spring onions, chopped, for garnish
1 red chilli, sliced, for garnish

1 In a food processor, grind the chickpeas to a smooth paste. Transfer to a mixing bowl.

2 Roast the sesame seeds in a dry frying pan for about 1 minute over a moderate heat, moving the pan constantly to toss the seeds around and prevent them from burning. Allow to cool briefly, then grind to a powder in a food processor.

3 Add the ground sesame seeds to the chickpeas, followed by the sugar, tamarind, green chillies and half the chopped coriander, with salt to taste. Process this mixture in the food processor briefly, in batches if necessary, until everything is well mixed.

4 Transfer to a serving bowl and garnish with the remaining coriander, chopped spring onions and red chilli.

PREPARATION
about 25 minutes
COOKING
2-3 minutes

Calories per serving *204*
Total fat *High*
Saturated fat *Low*
Protein *Low*
Carbohydrate *Low*
Cholesterol per serving *None*
Vitamins *B₁, B₆, Folate, C, E*
Minerals *Calcium, Potassium, Iron, Zinc*

DATE AND TAMARIND CHUTNEY

PREPARATION
about 10 minutes

Calories per serving *143*
Total fat *Low*
Saturated fat *Low*
Protein *Low*
Carbohydrate *High*
Cholesterol per serving
None
Vitamins *B₃*
Minerals *Potassium, Iron*

This chutney is easy to make and adds a sweet-and-sour flavour to any meal. Stoned and chopped dates are available at most supermarkets.

175 g / 6 oz stoned and chopped dates
1 tablespoon tamarind paste
1 tablespoon tomato ketchup
1 teaspoon ground coriander
1 teaspoon ginger powder

1 teaspoon chilli powder
1 teaspoon sugar
1 tablespoon chopped fresh mint
salt

1 Place all the ingredients in a food processor with 150 ml / ¼ pint water and salt to taste. Grind for about 1-1½ minutes, stopping halfway through to gather the mixture down from the sides.

2 Check to see it is smooth and transfer to a small serving bowl to serve. This chutney will keep for up to a week in the refrigerator.

PANIR

PREPARATION
*about 10 minutes,
plus 1½-2 hours'
setting*
COOKING
about 20 minutes

Calories per serving *116*
Total fat *Medium*
Saturated fat *High*
Protein *High*
Carbohydrate *Low*
Cholesterol per serving
18 mg
Vitamins *B₂, B₃, B₆, B₁₂,
Folate*
Minerals *Calcium,
Potassium, Zinc, Iodine*

This fresh cheese is an enduring ingredient in many Indian and Pakistani dishes. It is also often served as an extra dish, cut into cubes and swathed in a spicy tomato sauce like that for the Bombay Potatoes on page 132.

1 litre/ 1¾ pints semi-skimmed milk

2 tablespoons lemon juice

1 Bring the milk to the boil slowly over a low heat. Add the lemon juice, stirring continuously and gently until the milk thickens and begins to curdle. Strain the curdled milk through a sieve.

2 Set the strained curds aside between two

chopping boards and put a heavy weight on top for about 1½-2 hours to press to a flat shape about 1 cm / ½ inch thick.

3 Once set, the panir can be cut like any cheese, into whatever shape is required.

Slices of Panir served with Date and Tamarind Chutney, sliced red onion and mint sprigs

TOMATO AND ONION RAITA

SERVES 4

PREPARATION
about 10 minutes

Calories per serving *57*
Total fat *Medium*
Saturated fat *Low*
Protein *High*
Carbohydrate *Medium*
Cholesterol per serving
3 mg
Vitamins *B₂, B₃, B₆, B₁₂,*
Folate
Minerals *Calcium,*
Potassium, Iron, Zinc,
Iodine

Raitas *are served as accompaniments at most Indian meals, especially in Northern India. There are several types of* raita *and this is quite a popular one.*

300 ml / ½ pint plain low-fat runny yoghurt
1 onion, diced
2 tomatoes, diced
2 medium green chillies, diced
1 tablespoon chopped fresh coriander leaves
about ½ teaspoon sugar

salt

to garnish:
pinch of chilli powder
pinch of ground coriander

1   In a bowl, add to the low-fat yoghurt the diced onion, tomato, chillies, chopped fresh coriander, sugar and salt to taste. Mix everything together well and transfer the raita to a serving dish.

2   Garnish with the chilli powder and ground coriander to serve.

MINT AND MANGO RAITA

SERVES 4

PREPARATION
about 20 minutes

Calories per serving *82*
Total fat *Low*
Saturated fat *Low*
Protein *High*
Carbohydrate *High*
Cholesterol per serving
3 mg
Vitamins *A, B₂, B₃, B₆,*
Folate, C
Minerals *Calcium,*
Potassium, Iodine

A traditional raita *consists of yoghurt, mint, coriander and cucumber. There are a number of variations, however, and this particular one is rather unusual as I have used raw mango. It is certainly one of my favourites.*

300 ml / ½ pint plain low-fat runny yoghurt
1 mango
1 red chilli, diced
1 teaspoon mint sauce
½ cucumber, sliced

1 tablespoon clear honey
2 tablespoons chopped fresh coriander leaves
salt
few mint leaves, for garnish (optional)

1   Whisk the low-fat yoghurt well and place it in a serving bowl.

2   Peel the mango, cut it in half and remove the stone (see page 24). Cut the flesh coarsely and place it in the food processor. Add to this the chilli, mint sauce, cucumber, honey, coriander and salt to taste.

Grind all these ingredients briefly until the mixture is pulverized but not too smooth.

3   Empty the mixture into the yoghurt and gently stir together.

4   Garnish with mint leaves if you like, and serve.

Mint and Mango Raita

COCONUT AND CORIANDER CHUTNEY

Ideally you should use fresh coconut in this chutney. However, if this is difficult to find, you can use desiccated coconut.

PREPARATION
about 15 minutes

Calories per serving *191*
Total fat *High*
Saturated fat *High*
Protein *Low*
Carbohydrate *Low*
Cholesterol per serving
None
Vitamins *B₃, C*
Minerals *Iron*

125 g / 4½ oz grated fresh or desiccated coconut
1 green chilli, chopped
2 tablespoons chopped fresh mint

4 tablespoons chopped fresh coriander leaves
salt

1   Place the coconut in a food processor and add the chopped chilli, fresh mint, fresh coriander and salt to taste. Grind them together for about 2 minutes, stopping once to gather the mass together.

2   Remove from the processor and transfer to a small serving bowl. Use within a day or two.

MANGO AND COCONUT CHUTNEY

As before, although it is nice to use freshly grated coconut for this sweet-and-sour chutney, desiccated coconut will produce almost as tasty results.

1 large green mango
2 tablespoons chopped fresh coriander leaves
2 fresh green chillies, chopped
1 tablespoon grated fresh or desiccated coconut

about 1 teaspoon sugar
salt
½ red pepper, deseeded and chopped

1   Peel the mango and discard the stone. Cut the mango flesh into small pieces (see page 24).
2   Transfer the mango flesh to a food processor and add to this the chopped fresh coriander, chillies, desiccated coconut, sugar and salt to taste. Grind all the ingredients for about 1 minute or

until everything is quite finely chopped.
3   Pour in about 150-300 ml / ¼-½ pint of water to achieve the consistency of a thick paste. Transfer to a serving chutney dish and serve sprinkled with the chopped red pepper. Use promptly.

PREPARATION
about 20 minutes

Calories per serving *52*
Total fat *High*
Saturated fat *High*
Protein *Low*
Carbohydrate *Medium*
Cholesterol per serving *None*
Vitamins *A, C*
Minerals *Potassium*

QUICK MINT AND CUCUMBER RAITA

It is surprising how easy it is to make this delicious raita, *which is so versatile it can be served as an accompaniment to almost any meal.*

½ cucumber
300 ml / ½ pint plain low-fat runny yoghurt
salt
1 level teaspoon sugar

1 teaspoon mint sauce
1 fresh red chilli, diced
1 tablespoon chopped fresh coriander leaves
sprigs of fresh mint, to garnish

1   Peel the cucumber and finely dice the flesh.
2   Whisk the yoghurt in a bowl and add salt to taste, the sugar, mint sauce, chilli and coriander.

3   Finally, mix in the cucumber and transfer to a serving bowl. Serve garnished with the mint sprigs.

SERVES 4

PREPARATION
about 10 minutes

Calories per serving *53*
Total fat *Low*
Saturated fat *Low*
Protein *High*
Carbohydrate *Medium*
Cholesterol per serving *3 mg*
Vitamins B_2, B_3, B_{12}, *Folate*
Minerals *Calcium, Potassium, Iodine*

Desserts

TROPICAL FRUIT SALAD
WITH ROASTED ALMONDS

SERVES 4

PREPARATION
*about 20 minutes,
plus roasting the
almonds*

Calories per serving *388*
Total fat *Medium*
Saturated fat *Low*
Protein *Low*
Carbohydrate *High*
Cholesterol per serving
7 mg
Vitamins *A, B group, C, E*
Minerals *Calcium,
Potassium, Iron, Zinc*

2 large ripe mangoes
2 ripe papayas
*3 ripe guavas (use canned if fresh are not
available)*
8 black grapes, preferably seedless
8 white grapes, preferably seedless
1 Galia melon
1 small pineapple

2 bananas
1 red apple
2 fresh figs
2 kiwi fruits
1 tablespoon icing sugar
60 g / 2 oz almonds
225 g / 8 oz half-fat fromage frais (optional)

Previous pages: Tropical Fruit Salad with Roasted Almonds

1   Prepare the fruit (try to save all the juices as you work): remove the flesh from the mangoes (see page 24) and discard the stones and skin. Cut the papayas in half and scoop out the seeds. Peel and cut the flesh into chunks. Deseed the guavas if desired and scoop out chunks of the flesh with a spoon. Place all these in a serving bowl as they are ready.

2   Cut the grapes in half or leave them whole as you wish, and place these in the bowl as well. Cut the melon in half and scoop out the seeds. Using a melon baller or sharp-sided spoon, scoop out flesh in balls and add to the bowl.

3   Pare the skin from the pineapple, halve and remove the core. Slice thickly and then cut the slices into chunks. Peel the bananas, slice them and add to the bowl. Halve and core the apple, then cut into coarse chunks, add to the bowl. Pour over any captured juices and toss lightly to mix.

4   Cut the figs into quarters. Peel the kiwi fruits and slice them. Place the kiwi slices and fig quarters on top of the fruit salad and dust with some icing sugar. Put to chill briefly.

5   Meanwhile, toast the almonds in a dry frying pan over moderate heat, turning frequently and taking care they do not burn, until well coloured.

5   Serve the salad decorated with the roasted almonds and with the fromage frais if you are using it.

BASIC RICE PUDDING

Rice pudding is one of the most popular of Indian desserts, and most people make it on a regular basis at home.

1/2 cup basmati rice, well rinsed
1.25 litres / 2 pints semi-skimmed milk

2 tablespoons desiccated coconut, plus more for decoration (optional)
6-8 tablespoons sugar

1   Put the drained rice in a heavy-based saucepan Pour in half the milk and bring to the boil over a moderate heat. Leave to boil gently for 12-14 minutes, until soft (a wooden spoon in the pan helps prevent the milk boiling over).

2   When the rice is cooked, mash it down further in the milk using a wooden masher, if possible; otherwise just place half of it in a food processor and grind it down. Once the mixture is soft and mushy, add the coconut and blend it in well.

3   Pour in the remaining milk and bring to the boil again. Cook at a gentle boil for 2-3 minutes, or until it has the consistency of a thick creamy soup.

4   Finally stir in the sugar in and cook, stirring, for a further 2 minutes or so. Serve decorated with more desiccated coconut, if desired.

SERVES 4

PREPARATION
5 minutes
COOKING
about 20 minutes

Calories per serving *317*
Total fat *Medium*
Saturated fat *High*
Protein *Medium*
Carbohydrate *Medium*
Cholesterol per serving
22 mg
Vitamins B_1, B_2, B_3, B_6, B_{12},
Folate
Minerals *Calcium,*
Potassium, Zinc, Iodine

MANGO WITH SAFFRON
AND FROMAGE FRAIS

SERVES 4

PREPARATION
about 15 minutes

Calories per serving *193*
Total fat *Medium*
Saturated fat *Medium*
Protein *Low*
Carbohydrate *High*
Cholesterol per serving
13 mg
Vitamins *A, B group, C, E*
Minerals *Calcium,*
Potassium, Iron, Iodine

The taste of mangoes from the Indian subcontinent is quite something. The fruit is in season from around the middle of May until just before the monsoons at the end of July, and practically everyone looks forward to their arrival. Throughout the season, mangoes are eaten as desserts in many different ways; and, although mango pulp is available in cans, this recipe is best made using fresh mangoes.

4 large ripe mangoes
300 ml / ½ pint semi-skimmed milk
125 g / 4½ oz virtually fat-free fromage frais
¼ teaspoon saffron strands

1 tablespoon sugar
30 g / 1 oz mixed roasted flaked almonds and chopped pistachio nuts, to decorate (optional)

1 Remove the flesh from the mangoes and discard stones and skin (see page 24).

2 Place the mango flesh in a food processor together with the milk, fromage frais, saffron and

sugar. Process until the mixture is smooth.

3 Transfer this mixture to a serving bowl. Decorate with the almonds and pistachio nuts, if you wish.

WATERMELON AND PAPAYA JUICE

SERVES 2

PREPARATION
about 20 minutes

Calories per serving *87*
Total fat *Low*
Saturated fat *Low*
Protein *Low*
Carbohydrate *High*
Cholesterol per serving
None
Vitamins *A, C*
Minerals *Potassium, Iron*

When I was a child, my mother would give us this juice on a very hot day. It was probably the most refreshing drink I have ever enjoyed. Choose a nice red watermelon and a ripe but not overripe papaya.

1 small papaya
2 thick slices of watermelon
1 tablespoon sugar

1 teaspoon lemon juice
6-8 ice cubes, crushed

1 Cut the papaya in half and remove all the seeds. Peel the papaya and coarsely chop the flesh.

2 Remove the skin and as many seeds as possible from the watermelon. Chop the flesh coarsely.

3 Place the papaya, watermelon, sugar and lemon

juice in a liquidizer with 125 ml / 4 fl oz water. Liquidize for 1-1½ minutes, until smooth.

4 Pour the juice through a sieve into glasses filled with crushed ice.

Mango with Saffron and Fromage Frais, Watermelon and Papaya Juice

RICE PUDDING WITH CARDAMOM AND SAFFRON

SERVES 4

For special occasions serve this rather special and delicately flavoured rice pudding decorated with silver leaf.

PREPARATION
about 10 minutes
COOKING
25-30 minutes

Calories per serving *320*
Total fat *Medium*
Saturated fat *Medium*
Protein *Medium*
Carbohydrate *Medium*
Cholesterol per serving
22 mg
Vitamins *B₁, B₂, B₃, B₆,*
B₁₂, E
Minerals *Calcium*
Potassium, Iron, Zinc

3 tablespoons of basmati rice
1.25 litres / 2 pints semi-skimmed milk
cardamom seeds from 1 green cardamom pod
1 tablespoon ground almonds
6-8 tablespoons sugar
½ teaspoon saffron strands, lightly crushed

to decorate:
1 tablespoon flaked almonds
1 tablespoon ground pistachio nuts
silver leaf (optional)

1 Rinse the rice well, put it in a large heavy-based saucepan and add half the milk. Add the cardamom seeds and bring to the boil slowly over a very low heat, stirring occasionally. Cook for about 10 minutes, until all the milk has been absorbed by the rice, stirring occasionally.

2 Remove from the heat and mash the rice, preferably using a wooden masher and making swift round movements, for at least 5 minutes.

3 Return to the heat and add the ground almonds. Gradually stir in the remaining milk and bring to the boil, stirring occasionally.

4 Add the sugar and stir for a further 5-7 minutes, or until the pudding is quite thick.

5 Add the saffron strands and cook for a further minute before transferring it to a serving dish.

6 Garnish with the flaked almonds and ground pistachio nuts, and silver leaf if you wish.

SWEET POTATO DESSERT

SERVES 6-8

PREPARATION
15 minutes
COOKING
about 20 minutes

This delicious milky dessert can be eaten hot or cold.

900 g / 2 lb sweet potatoes
850 ml / 1½ pints semi-skimmed milk

115 g / 4 oz sugar
few flaked almonds to decorate (optional)

1   Peel the sweet potatoes. Using a sharp knife, cut them into slices.

2   Place the sweet potato slices in a large saucepan, cover with 600 ml / 1 pint of the milk and cook slowly until they are soft enough to be mashed.

3   Remove the pan from the heat and mash the sweet potatoes and milk well (preferably with a wooden masher) removing all the lumps.

4   Add the sugar and the remaining milk. Return to the heat and simmer gently until the mixture thickens. It should reach the consistency of a creamy soup.

5   Decorate the dessert with a few flaked almonds to serve, if you wish.

Calories per serving *207*
Total fat *Low*
Saturated fat *Low*
Protein *Low*
Carbohydrate *High*
Cholesterol per serving
7 mg
Vitamins *A, B group, C, E*
Minerals *Calcium,*
Potassium, Iodine

FRESH MANGO MILK SHAKE

Try to choose ripe mangoes for this recipe, it doesn't matter if they are slightly over-soft.

2 large ripe mangoes
sugar to taste

600 ml / 1 pint semi-skimmed or skimmed milk,
plus more if necessary

SERVES 2-3

PREPARATION
about 15 minutes,
plus chilling

1   Remove the flesh from the mangoes and discard the stones and skin (see page 24). Slice the flesh coarsely.

2   Put the mango in a liquidizer, together with sugar to taste and the milk. Process for about 1-1½ minutes. If it is too thick, add some more milk.

3   Transfer to 2-3 glasses and serve chilled.

Calories per serving *175*
Total fat *Low*
Saturated fat *Medium*
Protein *Medium*
Carbohydrate *High*
Cholesterol per serving
14 mg
Vitamins *A, B group, C, E*
Minerals *Calcium,*
Potassium, Iodine

MANGO AND PINEAPPLE JUICE DRINK

SERVES 2

PREPARATION
about 15 minutes

Calories per serving *132*
Total fat *Low*
Saturated fat *None*
Protein *Low*
Carbohydrate *High*
Cholesterol per serving
None
Vitamins *A, B₃, C, E*
Minerals *Potassium, Iron*

The sweet rich flavour of the mango and the slight sharpness of the pineapple give this drink a delicious tangy flavour, and it is a very cooling drink after a spicy meal.

2 large mangoes
½ pineapple

6-8 ice cubes, crushed

1 Remove the flesh from the mangoes and discard the stones and skin (see page 24). Slice the flesh coarsely.
2 Prepare the pineapple by removing the skin and cutting it into cubes.

3 Place the fruit in a food processor or liquidizer with half the crushed ice. Liquidize for about 1-1½ minutes until smooth, and serve with the remaining crushed ice stirred in.

MANGO DRINK COCKTAIL

SERVES 2

PREPARATION
about 10 minutes,
plus chilling

Calories per serving *122*
Total fat *Low*
Saturated fat *Medium*
Protein *Medium*
Carbohydrate *High*
Cholesterol per serving
9 mg
Vitamins *A, B₂, B₃, B₆,*
B₁₂, C
Minerals *Calcium,*
Potassium, Iodine

This drink could easily pass for a dessert. Serve it either at the end of a meal or during the course of it. Canned mango pulp is available at most Asian stores if you can't find fresh mangoes.

6-8 ice cubes, crushed
2 tablespoons mango pulp
1 teaspoon lemon juice
150 ml / ¼ pint plain low-fat runny yoghurt

1 tablespoon sugar
2 tablespoons low-fat vanilla ice-cream
mint sprigs, to decorate (optional)

1 Place the crushed ice in 2 long glasses and chill in the refrigerator.
2 Mix together the mango pulp, lemon juice,

yoghurt, sugar and ice-cream.
3 Pour this mixture over the crushed ice and serve decorated with mint sprigs if you wish.

Mango and Pineapple Juice Drink

CARDAMOM, PLUM AND APRICOT DESSERT

SERVES 4

PREPARATION
about 5 minutes
COOKING
20-25 minutes

Calories per serving *173*
Total fat *Low*
Saturated fat *Low*
Protein *Low*
Carbohydrate *High*
Cholesterol per serving
7 mg
Vitamins *A, B group*
Minerals *Potassium, Iron*

5 ripe red plums
5 apricots
2 cardamom pods
60 g / 2 oz sultanas

1 clove
4 tablespoons sugar
115 g / 4 oz low-fat fromage frais,
to serve (optional)

1 Peel the plums and apricots, halve them and remove the stones.

2 Place the plums and apricots in a pan with the cardamom pods, the sultanas, the clove and the sugar. Pour in 600 ml / 1 pint of water and stir well.

3 Bring to the boil, reduce the heat to moderate and cook for 15-20 minutes, or until the fruit is tender and the water has become syrupy.

4 Allow to cool a little and serve warm, with the fromage frais if you wish.

ZAFRANI SEVIAN
Saffron Vermicelli Pudding

SERVES 4

PREPARATION
about 5 minutes
COOKING
about 30 minutes

Calories per serving *224*
Total fat *Low*
Saturated fat *Low*
Protein *Medium*
Carbohydrate *High*
Cholesterol per serving
15 mg
Vitamins *B group*
Minerals *Calcium,*
Potassium, Iodine

850 ml / 1½ pints semi-skimmed milk
3 tablespoons crushed fine vermicelli
large pinch of saffron strands

30 g / 1 oz sultanas
4 tablespoons sugar
1 tablespoon toasted flaked almonds

1 Place the milk in a saucepan and add the vermicelli. Bring to the boil, then simmer gently for 15-20 minutes, until quite thick.

2 Stir in the saffron and simmer for about 7 minutes more, stirring occasionally, until the mixture has the consistency of a thick soup.

3 Stir in the sultanas and sugar and bring to a good rolling boil, briefly.

4 Transfer to a serving dish and serve decorated with the flaked almonds.

INDEX

Page numbers in *italic* refer to illustrations

almonds, 25-6
amchoor, 10
apple and mango chutney, *107, 130-31*, 139
apricots, 156
aubergines, 19
    courgettes and aubergines in a minty yoghurt sauce, 100-1
    with tomato and onion, 106, *107*
avocado with spicy lemon prawns, 40

balti tiger prawns with mushrooms, 62, *63*
barbecued marinated seafood, 46-7, 49
basmati rice, 28
    with chicken and vegetables, 67
bay leaves, 16
bay rice with peas, 118
black-eye beans, 22
    kachoomer with, 138
Bombay potatoes, *130-31*, 132
bread: chapati, 9, *75, 107, 122-3*, 124-5
    naan, *43, 45, 76, 92-3, 122-3*, 124
    roti, 125

cardamom, 10-12, 156
    cardamom, plum and apricot dessert, 156
cashew nuts, 26
cauliflower, 20
    trout with baby potatoes and, 54-5
    with peppers, 117
chana dhal, 23
    with panir and tomatoes, 116-17
chapati, 9, *75, 107, 122-3*, 124-5

chapati flour, 28
cheese *see* panir
chicken: baked coconut chicken with spicy mashed parsnip, 73
    basmati rice with vegetables and, 67
    char-grilled lemon chicken, 72
    chicken breasts with fruity saffron sauce, 83
    chicken breasts with mango sauce, 74, *75*
    chicken kadahi, 90
    fried chicken with fresh coriander and lemon, 82-3
    ginger and lemon chicken, 80, 81
    grilled chicken boti kebabs, 42, *43*
    grilled chicken kebabs, 72
    haleem, 70, *71*
    hot achaari chicken, 78
    hot and spicy chicken stir-fry with sesame, *76, 77*
    roast chicken quarters with a spicy honey sauce, 82
    roast chicken with lime and herbs, 78, *79*
    roast chicken with spicy mushrooms, 68, *69*
    spaghetti with mini chicken kofta, *86, 87*
    spiced roast poussin, *64-5*, 66
    tandoori chicken with radish salad, 84, *85*
    with fenugreek and tomatoes, 88, *89*
    see also liver
chickpeas, 22-3
    chickpea salad, 134, *135*
    chohlay, 36
    sweet-and-sour chickpea and sesame seed chutney, 139
chillies, 12, 17-19
    cod with mushrooms and, 50
chohlay, 36

chutneys: coconut and coriander, 144
    date and tamarind, 140, *141*
    mango and apple, 107, *130-31*, 139
    mango and coconut, 145
    sweet-and-sour chickpea and sesame seed, 139
cinnamon, 12
cloves, 12
coconut, 26
    baked coconut chicken with spicy mashed parsnip, 73
    coconut and coriander chutney, 144
    mango and coconut chutney, 145
    rice with desiccated coconut, *81*, 128
cod: cod fillets with spicy gram flour coating, 52
    masala grilled cod steaks, 38, *39*
    with mushrooms and green chillies, 50, *51*
coriander, 16-17
    coconut and coriander chutney, 144
    fried chicken with fresh coriander and lemon, 82-3
    mushroom and fresh coriander soup, 44, *45*
    plaice fillets with a creamy coriander topping, 52, *53*
coriander seeds, 12-13
courgettes and aubergines in a minty yoghurt sauce, 100-101
cracked wheat: haleem, 70, *71*
cucumber: quick mint and cucumber raita, *30-31*, 145
cumin, 13
curry leaves, 17

dairy products, 29
date and tamarind chutney, 140, *141*

dhals, 22-3
    doodhi, 20
    with moong dhal, 113, *114-15*
drinks, 150, 153-4

eggs: boiled egg curry, 112
equipment, 9

fennel seeds, 13
fenugreek, 13, 17
    chicken with tomatoes and, 88, *89*
    plaice fillets with a fenugreek sauce, 48
fish and shellfish, 46-62
flour, 28-9
fromage frais: mango with saffron and, 150, *151*
    spinach with garlic and, 120, *121*
fruit, 24-5
    tropical fruit salad, *146-7*, 148-9

garam masala, 13-14
garlic, 19
ghee, 29
ginger, 14, 19
    ginger and lemon chicken, 80, *81*
    lamb kebabs with a spicy ginger filling, 91
gram flour, 29
    roti, 125
green beans, 20
guavas, 24

haleem, 70, *71*
hara masala lamb kebabs, *64-5*, 94
herbs, 16-17

ingredients, 10-29

kachoomer with black-eye beans, 138

kadahi, 9
kebabs: grilled chicken, 72
    grilled chicken boti, 42, 43
    hara masala lamb, 64-5, 94
    lamb with a spicy ginger
        filling, 91
    potato with minced prawn
        filling, 33
    prawn and vegetable, 30-31,
        32
kewra water, 29
khicheri, masoor dhal with
    vegetables, 98-9, 100

lamb: hara masala kebabs, 64-5,
    94
    lamb kebabs with a spicy
        ginger filling, 91
    lamb pulao, 92-3, 94-5
    spring lamb chops with grilled
        vegetables, 92-3, 95
    stir-fried strips of lamb with
        peppers and pineapple, 96, 97
leek and potato soup with
    coriander, 44
lentils: masoor dhal khicheri
    with vegetables, 98-9, 100
    with vegetables and tamarind,
        102, 103
liver: chicken livers with spring
    onion, 41

mangoes, 24
    chicken breasts with mango
        sauce, 74, 75
    fresh mango milk shake, 153
    mango and apple chutney,
        107, 130-31, 139
    mango and coconut chutney,
        145
    mango drink cocktail, 15
    mint and mango raita, 142,
        143
    with saffron and fromage
        frais, 150, 151
masala grilled cod steaks, 38, 39
masala prawn and vegetable
    samosas, 37
masoor dhal, 23

masoor dhal khicheri with
    vegetables, 98-9, 100
meat and poultry, 64-96
milk shake, fresh mango, 153
mint, 17
    mint and mango raita, 142,
        143
    quick mint and cucumber
        raita, 30-31, 145
monkfish with garlic, 54, 56-7
mooli, 20
moong dhal, 23
    doodhi with, 113, 114-15
mushrooms: balti tiger prawns
    with, 62, 63
    cod with green chillies and, 50
    mushroom and fresh
        coriander soup, 44, 45
    roast chicken with spicy
        mushrooms, 68, 69
mustard seeds, 14

naan, 43, 45, 76, 92-3, 122-3, 124
nutmeg, 14
nuts, 25-6
    roasting, 8

okra, 20
    with baby potatoes, 98-9, 101
onion seeds, 14
onions: king prawn dopiaza
    with mango powder, 58, 59
    tomato and onion raita, 142
    tomato and onion salad, 130-
        31, 132

pancake roll, grilled vegetables
    in, 108, 109
panir, 29, 140, 141
    baked tomatoes stuffed with
        panir cubes and vegetables,
        110, 111
    chana dhal with tomatoes
        and, 116-17
    sweetcorn and peas with, 118,
        119
papaya, 24
    watermelon and papaya juice,
        150, 151

paprika, 14
parsnip, baked coconut chicken
    with spicy mashed, 73
pasta with prawns and sun-
    dried peppers, 60, 61
peas: aromatic rice with, 126,
    127
    bay rice with, 118
    prawns with red pepper and,
        58
    sweetcorn and peas with
        panir, 118, 119
    tamatar aur matar kay chawal,
        126
peppercorns, 14
peppers: cauliflower with, 117
    pasta with prawns and sun-
        dried peppers, 60, 61
    prawns with peas and red
        pepper, 58
    stir-fried strips of lamb with
        pineapple and, 96, 97
pine nuts, 26
    rice with, 128
pineapple, 24-5
    mango and pineapple juice
        drink, 154, 155
    stir-fried strips of lamb with
        peppers and, 96, 97
pistachio nuts, 26
plaice: lemon and garlic plaice,
    49
    plaice fillets with a creamy
        coriander topping, 52, 53
    plaice fillets with a fenugreek
        sauce, 48
plums: cardamom, plum and
    apricot dessert, 156
pomegranate seeds, 14-15
poppy seeds, 15
potatoes: Bombay potatoes,
    130-31, 132
    leek and potato soup with
        coriander, 44
    okra with baby potatoes, 98-9,
        101
    potato kebabs with minced
        prawn filling, 33
    potatoes in a sour sauce, 116

spicy potato and kidney bean
    salad, 133
spicy spinach and potato
    bake, 112-13, 114-15
trout with baby potatoes and
    cauliflower, 54-5
poultry and meat, 64-96
poussin, spiced roast, 64-5, 66
prawns: avocado with spicy
    lemon prawns, 40
    balti tiger prawns with
        mushrooms, 62, 63
    king prawn dopiaza with
        mango powder, 58, 59
    masala prawn and vegetable
        samosas, 37
    pasta with sun-dried peppers
        and, 60, 61
    potato kebabs with minced
        prawn filling, 33
    prawn and vegetable kebabs,
        30-31, 32
    shallot and king prawn
        starter, 34, 35
    with peas and red pepper, 58
pulao: lamb, 92-3, 94-5
    vegetable and red kidney
        bean, 104, 105
pulses, 22-3

radish salad, tandoori chicken
    with, 84, 85
raitas: mint and mango, 142,
    143
    quick mint and cucumber,
        30-31, 145
    tomato and onion, 142
red kidney beans, 23
    spicy potato and kidney bean
        salad, 133
    vegetable and red kidney bean
        pulao, 104, 105
rice, 28
    aromatic rice with peas, 126,
        127
    basic rice pudding, 149
    basmati rice with chicken and
        vegetables, 67
    bay rice with peas, 118

lamb pulao, *92-3*, 94-5
masoor dhal khicheri with vegetables, *98-9*, 100
rice pudding with cardamom and saffron, 152
saffron rice moulds, *64-5*, 129
spicy rice and vegetable stir-fry, 120
tamatar aur matar kay chawal, 126
vegetable and red kidney bean pulao, *104*, 105
with desiccated coconut, *81*, 128
with pine nuts, 128
roasting seeds, spices and nuts, 8
rose water, 29
roti, 125

saffron, 15
chicken breasts with fruity saffron sauce, 83
mango with fromage frais and, 150, 151
rice pudding with cardamom and, 152
saffron rice moulds, *64-5*, 129
saffron vermicelli pudding, 156
salads: chickpea, 134, *135*
with black-eye beans, 138
mixed salad with sweetcorn, 133
spicy potato and kidney bean, 133
spinach and sweet potato, 136, *137*
tandoori chicken with radish

salad, 84, *85*
tomato and onion, *130-31*, 132
samosas, masala prawn and vegetable, 37
seafood, barbecued marinated, *46-7*, 49
seeds, roasting, 8
sesame seeds, 15
hot and spicy chicken stir-fry with sesame, *76*, 77
sweet-and-sour chickpea and sesame seed chutney, 139
shallot and king prawn starter, 34, 35
shellfish and fish, 46-62
silver leaf, 29
soups, 44
spaghetti with mini chicken kofta, *86*, 87
spices, 10-15
grinding, 8
roasting, 8
spinach, 20
spicy spinach and potato bake, 112-13, *114-15*
spinach and sweet potato salad, 136, *137*
with garlic and fromage frais, 120, *121*
spring onions, chicken livers with, 41
stir-frying, 8-9
sweet-and-sour chickpea and sesame seed chutney, 139
sweet potatoes, 22
spinach and sweet potato salad, 136, *137*

sweet potato dessert, 153
sweetcorn: mixed salad with, 133
sweetcorn and peas with panir, 118, *119*

tamarind, 15
date and tamarind chutney, 140, *141*
lentils with vegetables and, 102, *103*
tamatar aur matar kay chawal, 126
tandoori chicken with radish salad, 84, *85*
thawa, 9
tomatoes: aubergine with onion and, 106, *107*
baked tomatoes stuffed with panir cubes and vegetables, 110, *111*
chicken with fenugreek and, 88, *89*
tamatar aur matar kay chawal, 126
tomato and onion raita, 142
tomato and onion salad, *130-31*, 132
trout-filled beef tomatoes, 40
toor dhal, 23
tropical fruit salad, *146-7*, 148-9
trout: baked trout with spicy almond and coconut sauce, 55, *56-7*
trout-filled beef tomatoes, 40
with baby potatoes and cauliflower, 54-5
turmeric, 15

unleavened bread, 124-5
urid dhal, 23

vegetables, 19-22
grilled vegetables in a pancake roll, 108, *109*
hot and spicy chicken stir-fry with sesame, *76*, 77
lentils with tamarind and, 102, *103*
masoor dhal khicheri with, *98-9*, 100
prawn and vegetable kebabs, *30-31*, 32
spicy rice and vegetable stir-fry, 120
spring lamb chops with grilled vegetables, *92-3*, 95
vegetable and red kidney bean pulao, *104*, 105

vermicelli: saffron vermicelli pudding, 156

watermelon and papaya juice, 150, *151*
wheat *see* cracked wheat

yeasted bread, 124
yoghurt, 29
courgettes and aubergines in a minty yoghurt sauce, 100-1
mint and mango raita, 142, *143*
quick mint and cucumber raita, *30-31*, 145
tomato and onion raita, 142

ACKNOWLEDGMENTS

The author would like to express her grateful thanks to her mother for her continued support, her love for her husband and many thanks to her children Humaira, Sumra and Asim, wishing them all a long, happy and healthy life.

Ameen

Editor and Project Manager: Lewis Esson
Photographic Styling: Antonia Gaunt
Food Styling: Janet Smith
Nutritional Analysis: Patricia Bacon
Indexer: Hilary Bird
Page Make-up: Clive Dorman & Co
Production: Peter Hinton
Commissioning Editor: Jo Christian
Art Editor: Louise Kirby
Contributing Editor: Sarah Mitchell
Assistant Editor: Kirsty Brackenridge
Picture Editor: Anne Fraser
Editorial Director: Erica Hunningher
Art Director: Caroline Hillier